A CALL
TO THE
SECRET PLACE

A CALL
TO THE
SECRET PLACE

By Michal Ann Goll

Treasure House

An Imprint of

Destiny Image® Publishers, Inc.
P.O. Box 310
Shippensburg, PA 17257-0310

"For where your treasure is, there will your heart be also."
Matthew 6:21

ISBN 0-7684-2179-9

For Worldwide Distribution
Printed in the U.S.A.

This book and all other Destiny Image, Revival Press, MercyPlace, Fresh
Bread, Destiny Image Fiction, and Treasure House books are available at
Christian bookstores and distributors worldwide.

For a U.S. bookstore nearest you, call **1-800-722-6774**.
or more information on foreign distributors, call **717-532-3040**.
Or reach us on the Internet:

www.destinyimage.com

ENDORSEMENTS

In her new book, *A Call to the Secret Place*, Michal Ann Goll has captured the essence of what the good news of Jesus Christ is all about. The secret place spoken of in Psalm 91:1 is hard to find but oh, so rewarding when we find it. The examples she uses of spiritual warriors are very touching and heartwarming. She has expressed what many of us feel—a yearning in our hearts to know our Savior better. I recommend this book to anyone who wants to find that secret place next to the heart of God.

—Evelyn Roberts
Wife of Oral Roberts

I believe the message of this book is both timely and prophetic for the days we are living in. It is in the place of intimacy with the Lord where we are changed into His likeness. It is in the place of intimacy that His power and anointing begin to flow through us in the most wonderful ways. I encourage you to live out the message of this book and watch your life be radically transformed.

—Carol Arnott, Senior Pastor
Toronto Airport Christian Fellowship

Michal Ann Goll has written beautifully calling us to the secret place. With many anecdotes and examples from both the past and the present from those who made it to the secret place, Michal Ann is calling us to follow in their foot steps. I believe she is articulating the call of the Holy Spirit, that He wants for all of us to enter into deeper intimacy.

—Wesley and Stacey Campbell
Revival Now! Ministries

Contents

Foreword

FOREWORD

A few months before I received the enlightening book you are holding in your hand, I was in Nashville, sitting in an intercessory prayer meeting just minutes before a women's conference was to begin. Seated on my left was Michal Ann Goll, the author of this book. On my right sat Beth Alves, one of the featured speakers and a subject of one of the chapters in this book.

I listened intently as they prayed aloud, since that's one of the ways I've learned to pray—tuning in as godly men and women commune with Him. As soon as Michal Ann began the prayer session, I felt a sense of God's presence sweep into our room. The air was almost electric. Here was a woman who communicates with the Lord so regularly and intimately, I knew her prayers had gone straight to His throne room. Once more, I believed He was going to answer her prayer for the conference to have His anointing and bring Him glory.

Beth, described by Michal Ann as "The Grandma of the Prayer Shield," prayed boldly and with fresh insights in her calm, expectant voice. I've known her many years and have been greatly encouraged by her prayers. Yet this morning her prayer was packed with great fervor and passion. She too had touched God's heart.

I joined my prayers with theirs. Then I thanked God silently for the privilege to be sitting beside these modern-day praying women!

That's how I think you will respond when you read this book. You will feel that you are not only in God's presence, but that you are coming to know personally the women "saints" Michal Ann writes about. While some lived several hundred years ago, others are contemporary women who have responded to God's call to the secret place.

All experienced more intimacy with Jesus through their prayer lives. All underwent hardship or persecution.

As Michal Ann so beautifully weaves their stories throughout her book, you too will have a desire to retreat—to enter the quiet sanctuary where God abides. You will yearn to open yourself more to His voice, His direction, His love.

As you do, I believe you will see glorious answers to prayer as we did at that Nashville conference.

Her previous book, *Women on the Front Lines*, greatly impacted many readers, including me. This new one about women of prayer makes you yearn to follow them on a journey of intimate communication with the Lord—abandoning yourself to His call.

Yes, He is calling us!

Get ready to be blessed and challenged as you ponder the lessons God wants to teach you through the life experiences of these dedicated women.

Quin Sherrer, Author
Miracles Happen When You Pray

SECTION ONE

"COME UP HERE"

CHAPTER 1

WHEN I'M CALLING YOU

I love that the gospel is so simple and real. God loves us so much; it's as though He has purposed to leave us love notes everywhere! Wherever we open our hearts to see and hear Him, He is there. It's wonderful to look back over your life and see those hidden messages strategically placed—especially when you haven't noticed them earlier.

I have one such love note I'd like to share with you. When I was growing up, my family had a few movie favorites that we truly enjoyed watching together. My parents just loved Jeanette MacDonald and Nelson Eddy movies. Jeanette MacDonald was believed to be a Christian and had a beautiful operatic voice. She sang in all her movies—at least the ones I saw. When her lovely voice was blended with Nelson Eddy's rich baritone one, the musical match was just heavenly.

One such movie was "Indian Love Call" (also known as "Rose-Marie"). The setting of this movie takes place in Canada; it is a romantic love story between a Canadian Royal Mounted police officer and a professional opera singer.

At one point, the couple stands at a breathtaking scenic high point in the Canadian mountains, looking down into the valley. The Mountie teaches a bit of Indian folklore by singing a song entitled, "Indian Love Call." The song captures the singer's heart, and they fall deeply in love.

When a conflict occurs that threatens to separate the lovers forever, Jeanette MacDonald returns to the mountain peak. Hoping that her voice will be able to find him, tearfully she sings "Indian Love Call" into the depths of the valley below. Her love is expressed in every line. As she sings, the sound of her voice echoes through the valley to the mountain on the other side. The hills echo back each note, each word...

> *When I'm calling you—*
> *Will you answer true?*
> *That means I'm offering my love to you—*
> *To be your own.*
> *If you refuse me, I will be blue—*
> *And waiting all alone.*
>
> *But, if when you hear my love call ringing clear,*
> *And I hear your answering echo, so dear.*
> *Then I will know our love will come true.*
> *You belong to me.*
> *I belong to you!*

Wow! Just typing those words brings such warmth and tenderness into my heart, because I now can see something in those words that I didn't see as a child. I hear a Voice calling me, and asking for a response to a song I've been taught by the greatest romantic of them all! If you listen, you'll hear it, too. Can you hear Him sing your name over the mountaintops? He is aching to hear your voice, your heart response to

Him. "When I'm calling you...Will you answer true...?" He's calling!

If we learn to listen, if we are still, we will hear the Voice that calls each one of us. And if we follow, we will find the secret place where the One who is love eternal dwells. There alone will we find strength and peace in His everlasting arms. There we'll be shown the wonders of His love.

The question is: How do we find our way to the secret place where God abides?

"Selah"

Today, we're learning great lessons about prayer. Many powerful ministries have sprung up, teaching us how to be prayer warriors; how to pray for the lost, our schools, our towns and cities, and our nation. Yet, for all our praying, many of us lack a sense of the closeness and intimacy with God we crave. Many of us pray but have no clue how to *find God in our* prayer time. With all our understanding about God's awesome power, it's as if we've lost sight of God Himself and His longing to be intimate with us.

If we want to find God in our everyday experience and sense His real presence throughout all life's struggles and joys, we must learn about a kind of prayer few of us understand. I am speaking about the prayer of inner quiet.

In the psalms, we discover long lists of God's amazing attributes and His great and mighty acts. We read, "You are the God who does wonders." "You have demonstrated Your power among the people." "With Your mighty arm You have redeemed Your people, the sons of Jacob and Joseph." We get into the pace of those words, imagining a God who is always on the move. Unfortunately, often we miss the all-important instruction at the end: "selah"—*pause a minute and calmly think about what you've just read.*

"Pause. Think about Me." In this tender instruction we hear the echo of God's voice calling to us from out of time. Calling us apart to be alone with Him. Throughout our busy days, we run until we drop and then get up the next day and start all over again.

Sadly, although we often complain about our demanding, stressed-out lives, most of us have become accustomed to the frantic pace. We scarcely know what to do with ourselves when things slow down. Some of us are even afraid to slow down, afraid because we know what will happen. We know that we've been running, running, running—keeping just ahead of the wind at our backs. And if we suddenly stop, the whirlwind of promises we've made and responsibilities we've picked up—everything that's swirling in our wake—will catch up with us. We've kept just a step ahead, but in a moment it could suddenly overtake us from behind. In truth, we ourselves have created these high-pressured lives, and still we ask, "*Where did all these demands and all this stress come from?*"

At the same time, we sense our own desire to retreat to the wonderful place in spirit, to enter the quiet sanctuary where God abides. We may even sense His call. But we become even more frustrated because of the seemingly increased demand someone is placing on us and our crammed schedules. Isn't that often our first objection when someone encourages us to give prayer a greater space in our lives? "I don't have the *time.*" We give up in frustration before we even start, and we never answer God's love-call.

Be Patient With Yourself

No matter how busy your lifestyle, no matter how stressed you've been, you can learn how to enter the secret place with God and know His real presence with you every day.

I want to say from the outset: Be patient with yourself. Learning to change the lifestyle you've been living is going to take time. At the same time, you will also need to learn how to be patient waiting upon God. Although God is always present with us, coming into the secret place with Him is one thing you cannot hurry. You're not going to get there if you're a speed-reader, or if you're a great administrator who lives by a checklist. None of the things you know how to do to "make things happen" will help you come into this place in spirit.

No matter who you are, you'll only find your way to the secret place with God if you learn to take the time.

Nothing Is Impossible

I can hear your objection, "I don't *have* time."

I assure you, I know all about the issue of time... and the lack thereof.

Some years ago, my husband, Jim, came home on fire after being at a fantastic Christian conference. He could hardly sit down. He walked from room to room, reviewing all the amazing details. "God was so great!" he kept saying. "*This* amazing thing happened, and *that* miracle took place."

All the while I was thinking, Please!—*don't tell me another word*. You see, at the time we were between houses, living with our four kids in someone else's basement. I was home-schooling a first grader and getting up in the night with our youngest, besides keeping up with the two in between.

Every ounce of energy and focus was going to the kids. I was so hungry to be with God, but I didn't have time to go off to a weekend retreat. Jim was so elated, and all I could do was listen and feel miserable.

When Jim finally left the room I leaned my head against the wall and silently cried, my tears releasing to God the depth of my hunger. I felt desperate, because it seemed that I could do nothing to find a spare minute to be alone with Him.

Just then the Lord came to me in my desperation, and in that still small voice inside He said, "Michal Ann, I'm God of the impossible. What's impossible for you is not impossible for Me. I'm going to start coming and visiting you in the night season."

I wasn't even sure I understood what He meant. But the most amazing thing began to happen. Night after night I began to dream. One night I dreamed a dear, sweet, old gentleman came to me. I knew who He was at once. He was so kind and loving, and He loved the fragrance of my hair. He wanted me to simply lean near and hug Him, so He could smell its fragrance. I'd never noticed that my hair had any kind of scent, but He did. He knew everything about me. In this way, night after night, God came wooing. We went on long walks, down country lanes, and He told me about the preciousness of my life and revealed how cherished I am. I was given a gift of seeing myself through His loving eyes!

Yes, I believe that perhaps these dreams were, in a way, unusual. But in no way do I think I am unique, or specially favored by God more than anyone else. He had a specific way of revealing His love to me at that time, and He has a very special, most wonderful way to reveal Himself to you, too.

I'm telling you about my experience so that you will know one thing for sure: With God, nothing is impossible. Even though you may feel like your schedule is too full or too busy, and you don't know how you can squeeze out an additional moment, God Himself can make a way. In fact, He is already seeking out the times and places where He can meet alone with you. He's looking for the tiniest opening in your day or your night, when He can make His wonderful presence known in a unique way in your life.

Entering In

Yes, the dream gave me assurance of God's love and presence. No, the dream did not last. It was a catalyst...or an invitation. It spurred me on to seek God, because suddenly I knew that intimacy with Him was absolutely possible—no matter where I was, no matter what kind of stress I was experiencing. I wish staying in that wonderful secret place with Him happened automatically, but it did not. Since then I've learned that we have to take practical steps to meet with the God who so obviously longs to meet with us.

How do we begin?

First, most of us have to disregard the idea that we have to be "specially called" to times of prayer. When we read First Thessalonians 5:17, where Paul tells us to "pray without ceasing," we might think that prayer is meant only for "super saints." Maybe some people are gifted in a way in which they can repeat their prayer lists all the time. Or, maybe we've grown up with a distorted view of what prayer really is! Maybe we're trying to approach prayer as a form of mental exercise— something that in our own natural power we can "do."

The fact is that God calls every one of us to prayer. The thing we must realize, however, is this: *Before God calls us to prayer, He calls us to Himself*. When God says, "Come away, MY beloved" (see Song 8:14a), He is calling every one of us. *He is calling you*.

Second, we need to find a place to be entirely alone. Susanna Wesley literally had no place to go inside her own home to get away from her many children in order to be alone with the Lord. So when she pulled her apron up over her head, her children knew it was time to leave her alone. Most of us have better living circumstances than Susanna Wesley. If you have a bathroom, or even a large closet, you can find a place to be alone.

Third, we must also learn what it takes to quiet our own spirit. Because we're so bombarded by outside noise and information, we don't even know what we ourselves are like on the inside and we can get totally out of touch with our own feelings and motives. We must begin to be quiet by disconnecting from the newspaper, the TV, the radio, and gab sessions with friends. We can then take time to search our hearts, with the help of the Holy Spirit, to find out what's really going on inside of us. Sometimes, we don't even want to know what's going on "in there." But if we want to find the secret place with God, we must enter with our true selves. Keeping up false fronts and masks will hinder us from experiencing God's presence. As David says in his great psalm of confession, only truth and honesty in the inward parts will allow us to enter where God abides (see Ps. 51:6).

Fourth, we need help to prevent our minds from wandering. If you've ever tried to spend time alone with the Lord, you know what I mean. You seek quiet and a break—but the minute you sit down "the list" takes over your mind. You think, *I can't just sit here. There's wet laundry in the dryer, and I've got to pay this bill, and... and... and....* You realize you're not getting anywhere spiritually, and you give up.

For this reason, I recommend you enter into the secret place with God by meditating on His Word. I can think of no better way to corral and direct your straying thoughts than to guide them along the spiritual pathways of truth laid out by God's Spirit. And of course, it is also important that we meditate on God's Word because through His Word, God builds up our faith by revealing Himself to us. There, in His Word, we see Him at work; we learn about His nature and character. We see Him act; we sense Him loving and winning back the world, and us, to Himself.

In each of these steps, we turn our hearts toward God. Each one makes possible the *fifth* thing we can do to prepare ourselves to meet with Him in the secret place; we must open ourselves to receive His love.

The strongest need we possess is our need to be loved. Most arguments we have with each other have to do with the issue of being loved. We each have inside us this huge vacuum that no human being can ever fill. Only God can fill the void we have within.

In order for God to fill us, our hearts must be wide open to Him—*yielded* to Him. Therefore, it's absolutely necessary that we learn to pray from our hearts. Praying from our heads, with our understanding, doesn't accomplish anything; because prayer is nothing more and nothing less than turning our heart fully toward God, opening up all of what we are to Him, and in turn receiving His love in place of our emptiness.

Opening to God, and yielding, is so difficult for many of us. What is it like to yield to Him? Consider Adam, just after he was created. There he was, a fine physical specimen made by God, perfect in every way. Yet there was no life in him. As Adam lay there on the ground, God bent down and was the One who breathed life into Adam. God is still doing that today, stopping to breathe life into our empty, needy souls. What did Adam do to receive this life? Nothing. He just lay there and let God do the breathing. In the same way, we must open ourselves to God, yield to Him, and simply allow Him to fill us.

Although I say "simply" allow God to fill you, it is a difficult instruction for us to grasp. We have such a works-mentality built into us. We mentally carry around lists of the many things we must do to become worthy. Unfortunately, the Christian Church can add to this pressure, making us feel that we need to do more to please God so that He will be "happy" with us. When in actuality, all that we are required to do is relax and breathe—just breathe in the breath, the very Spirit, of God who is always present with us.

And not only is He present with us, but there's also something even better...

"My Kingdom Is Within You."

When Jesus was promising the disciples that He would send the Holy Spirit so they wouldn't be left alone without Him after His death, He said,

*You know Him, for he lives with you **and will be in you*** (John 14:17b, emphasis added).

God Himself lives in you! His Kingdom, the place where He rules and reigns, is inside of you.

Prayer is surely about storming the heavenlies to tear down strongholds (see 2 Cor. 10:4), and prayer is about asking for our daily needs (see Mt. 6:11); but do you know about the kind of prayer that allows you to enter into the Kingdom of God, the presence of God, that has been deposited in you? Do you know the comfort of the Comforter who lives right within you? Or do you, like so many other Christians much of the time, wonder where God is in your life? Do you wonder what He's doing inside to transform you, and how you can know for sure He loves and cares about you through all life's trials?

This is an incredible fact—the Kingdom of God is within us, making God Himself accessible to us at any time.

Many truly great women of faith down through the ages have understood how to enter into that secret place with God. They have learned how to draw spiritual strength and courage from the depths of the inner man to face the hard times all around them. It's in the secret place of prayer that we find inspiration for the dull and dry times and comfort for the lonely and hurting times. Such mighty, truly noble Christian women knew how to exhale the concerns that sought to bind them as well as the misconceptions about God that might have kept them from approaching Him. They understood what it meant to empty themselves of all worldly preoccupations that can fill up the inner rooms of our souls and push Him out. They also knew how to relax into, and breathe in, His very presence. They knew what it meant to inhale the peace that only comes from Him, like a spiritual fragrance—and then to pray, "Father, I want to meet with You in the secret place."

Prayer is as simple as breathing out, asking God to clear out the clutter and the noise within, asking Him to create that inner room where you can always go to meet with Him in secret.

Have you learned what it's like to have God's very presence fill you the way breath fills your lungs? You can easily enter into the secret place of your soul where God's Spirit dwells if you know the way.

The kind of prayer I am referring to is not about getting it right or about achieving a goal, the motivation for many of our prayers; neither is it about making yourself presentable to God before you ask to meet with Him. There is a kind of intimate praying that can *only* come about as we learn to strip away pretense and come, just as we are, into the inner chamber with our Lord and King.

Some of us look at other Christian women, especially "prayer warriors" or "great women of faith" and think, *If only I knew how to pray the way **she** prays.* Unfortunately, we engage in a kind of worldly thinking when it comes to prayer. We treat prayer as if we're going into another woman's home to see her decorating scheme and lovely fabrics, furniture selection and colors. We think, *If only I could deck myself out like her.*

If only I could come before God the way she does—then my life with God would take off and my prayers would become powerful.

Prayer that brings us into intimate experiences with God does not involve imitating another or reproducing their prayers. You are your own person; you are unique. And there is a place of intimacy with you that God cannot find with anyone else. He wants you to have a relationship with Him that no one else can enjoy. *And so God wants you to be just exactly who you are.*

One of the greatest spiritual problems many of us have is wishing we were someone else. We want to enjoy God's presence, but we think, *God You really don't want to meet with me, do You?* Sister in Christ, God wants you to know that you can take yourself as you find yourself, and start from there. You can't change your history; you can't change mistakes or undo wrong things from your past. *You can't re-make yourself into somebody you're not.* So begin with the person you are today. Beginning with God is like standing in front of a sign in the mall that says, "You are here." God wants you to say, "God, I'm here! Just as I am, I come."

Being able to enter into the deep love and peace of God in prayer is not about getting rid of flaws and faults. If it were, we would spend all our time trying to make ourselves perfect, and that never works. Instead, it's being in the presence of Someone—the wonderful God who has said, "I am with you always..." (Mt. 28:20b). Entering your secret place requires nothing more than coming, for He says, "Everything and everyone that the Father has given Me will come to Me, and I won't turn any of them away" (Jn. 6:37 CEV).

The only requirement for finding our way to the secret place with God is just to begin. We begin by abandoning ourselves to God, which means seeking Him and learning to rest in His divine presence no matter what our circumstances.

If we abandon ourselves to God, we train our souls to rest in Him. We trust that He is in control of our lives, not only when everything goes well, but also when everything goes wrong. We trust that He has not abandoned us, and that He knows what's best for us by allowing different situations and circumstances into our lives. We make a deliberate choice to believe that He is working something bigger into us than what we can accomplish ourselves. I am not saying this is easy. It's not. But by abandoning ourselves to God and totally laying down our lives, we leave all our cares and concerns in His loving hands.

The Narrow Way

If we want the peace of God that only He can give, we must abandon ourselves completely to Him. Abandonment is the key that unlocks our entry to the secret place where our King and heavenly Bridegroom dwells.

Abandonment is the means God uses to reveal His mysteries to us. There are so many mysteries about God, which He longs to reveal to us His Bride. One of the greatest mysteries is the way God transforms us from who we are now into women who bear the marks of Jesus Christ. Paul referred to this mystery when he said in Galatians 6:17b, "I bear on my body the marks of Jesus." If we love and abandon ourselves to God, as Paul did, we will be transformed into His image.

I believe that Paul was describing the "narrow way" (see Mt. 7: 13–14), a way that stands open before each one of us. To find your way to this place in God requires giving Him the keys to everything: children, husbands, families, homes, possessions, friends, jobs, and our dreams. We must place everything into His hands and leave it there for Him to do with as He sees fit.

What will it take to produce this kind of abandonment in us? It does not come easily, and it takes great faith. The greater our faith, the more we know God, and the better we know Him, the easier it will be to abandon ourselves freely without the slightest hesitation or holding back.

Great Women of God Show Us the Way

What Jesus said is eternal truth: God is our center, and His Kingdom is within us (see Lk. 17:21).

When we become completely united with Him spirit, soul, and body (see 1 Thess. 5:23), the barriers of doubt, fear, and pride will all melt in the warmth of His love. We will come into a place where peace, love, and eternal strength are ours because we are one with Him, peacefully resting in the wonder of that love.

Throughout history, great men and women alike have found their way into the secret place where God dwells. They have entered that place by learning the secrets of quiet prayer, and how to abandon themselves completely to God. They knew how to become His Bride, and were consumed with the love and presence of God as they yielded themselves completely and became one with Him. In this book, we'll look at the lives of a few of these amazing women. We can learn much from them about answering God's call to the secret place.

As we begin, I offer this prayer on your behalf:

Father, lead us out of the storms and stresses of life that distract us and keep us from knowing You. More than anything else, we want to know You. We want to open our hearts and our lives wide open to You. Guide us by Your precious Holy Spirit to the secret place...where You can reveal Yourself in wonder, majesty, and holiness, in us and through us to a lost world. In Jesus' name, Amen.

Chapter 2

The Depths of God

~

"Come up here!" (Rev. 4:1b CEV).

When Jesus Christ calls you into the secret place of prayer, it's an invitation like no other. That call from the depths of God's presence is an unspeakable privilege, an open door to a revelation of God Himself. My one major goal in life is to be like the apostle John and answer the call of God to come into the secret place. What about you?

In the Book of Revelation, the veil is pulled back for a moment and we are afforded a glimpse of what John saw when he was called into the secret place. The apostle tells us: "On the Lord's Day I was in the Spirit, and I heard behind me a loud voice..." (Rev. 1:10).

When John turned to see who was calling, he was amazed! The One who commanded his attention was none other than Jesus. But it was not the Jesus he'd seen before— the itinerant Jewish rabbi in a robe and sandals. Here was the shining, resurrected Son of God, summoning John to come up with Him in the glorious heavenly sanctuary where He stood in the midst of fiery candlesticks. From His feet to His hair He was a blazing fire, so that "His face was like the sun shining in all its brilliance" (Rev. 1:16b)!

John was so overcome by this shining revelation of God that he "fell at His feet as a dead man" (Rev. 1:17a NAS). But Jesus placed His right hand on John, and lifted him up...and then He unfolded one of the greatest revelations of God that mankind has ever received.

I want to meet with Jesus Christ in the secret and holy place where He dwells in Spirit and, like John, be taken into the depths of God. I want to be a vessel that reveals the awesome mysteries of God's grace and truth to the world. Isn't that the greatest goal of your life, too?

Battle...and Blessing

The problem for most of us is that life crowds out the time we need to spend alone answering God's call. For example, one Sunday morning I was trying to find ten minutes to be alone with God, but it seemed that it was not to be! I went into this room, and I was followed. So I went into that room, and I was followed into that room, too. At every step, one child or another was coming to me saying, "Mom, I need this," or "Can we do that?"

I was doing my best to see them merely as innocent children, and I was trying to maintain a good attitude, but I felt bombarded. I kept thinking, *Why is it such a battle to get to the blessing?*

Interestingly I've learned that God is not absent from such circumstances. In fact, God is actually very present in these circumstances, allowing them to happen for a reason.

He grants us an opportunity to see who we really are spiritually as we're being pressed. He doesn't set up these situations to hurt, crush, destroy, or keep us away from Himself. He allows such circumstances, in part, so that we are able to see aspects of ourselves that we wouldn't otherwise see. Even though our human natures aren't eager to acknowledge the parts of us that God wants to transform, getting us to see them is a first step in helping us to understand that we need transformation, which means that we must endure the fires of trial and testing.

You see, our circumstances do not prevent God from being with us. Think about the children of Israel whom Nebuchadnezzar had thrown into a fiery furnace (see Dan. 3). Neither the wrath of an evil king nor roaring hot flames could prevent God from being with these godly men. Looking at the glowing core of deadly fire, Nebuchadnezzar was shocked to see one who "looks like a son of the gods" (Dan. 3:25b), walking in the flames with His faithful servants.

Our God is God. It makes no difference what circumstances surround us; He can still meet with us, and He can still provide for our every need.

I am writing this to you, not because I merely *hope* that it's true or because it sounds like the spiritual thing to say. I'm writing to tell you, as one who has received the true grace of God, that there is a way into the secret place where He dwells—*even in the midst of whatever kind of bombardment or fiery furnace you are going through*. The way is not to try to escape the flames, but to go through them.

Let me tell you how I learned this truth.

My Own Personal Fire

Today was just so awesome with God. Yes my kids were still being kids and my husband still needed me to take care of various things for him. But, in the midst of all that was going on around me, I was able to walk in the burning presence of God.

From this place of spiritual intimacy, the Lord is redeeming my past. He is showing me things that I hadn't understood before—events from the past that were hurtful to me, times when I felt spiritually dry, and long stretches in which I felt alone, forgotten, left out, and overlooked. How is He redeeming those times? He is revealing His plan and purpose for those very rough places I have gone through. Now that I am beginning to see through His perspective, I am realizing anew and afresh how I have never been apart from His great love for me. I have certainly not "arrived" spiritually. But I've moved beyond the unpleasant place where I felt stuck for many years.

In order to leave uncertainty and enter a new, peaceful place of assurance in His love I had to go through some very hot flames of testing.

For many years, I was at home all the time, and everyone knew me only as Jim Goll's wife or "the pastor's wife." Sometimes it's difficult to live with a person who is really well-known and liked. For some people, that person may be a spouse, for others it's a parent or sibling, and for others it may be a coworker. It can be even more difficult if you're the one who's holding down the fort!

People would call our home and say, "Oh, you have the most wonderful husband. His meetings are so awesome, and he is so anointed! You must feel so blessed to be married to him."

While I agreed with them, because Jim is an awesome vessel of God's grace and truth, still, something in my heart wanted to say, "But what about me? Where is the affirmation I need to feel valued for my contribution to 'our' ministry?" I felt like nothing more than an appendage. Sure, we can insist that we're spiritual people and we only want to please God. Yet, if we're really honest we must admit that we all want to be known and feel valued and respected for our labors.

What made it worse in those early years was our desperate desire to have children, but inability to conceive. I was barren for seven years, but then God dramatically and miraculously touched and healed me. I was absolutely ecstatic and filled with indescribable wonder and thanksgiving!

My pregnancy with Justin, our oldest, went well, except for some mild morning sickness in the early months. Then, during my second pregnancy with our daughter, Grace Ann, I became very, very ill. I spent months lying in bed. I was too sick and weak to even hold up my Bible because it was too heavy. I couldn't eat anything; I could barely keep down a tablespoon of liquid at a time. I looked terminally ill. It was truly by the grace of God that Grace Ann was born weighing 9 pounds 6 ounces, a totally healthy baby.

My system was so depleted; my body was worn out! Shortly thereafter, I became pregnant with our son Tyler. Again, I became very ill, not quite as bad, but serious enough that I lay in bed for months. My stomach would over-generate digestive juices that were eating me up from the inside out.

And so it went through the births of three of our four children. I was searching for purpose, value, and meaning, but I was left alone. I didn't see anybody. I didn't talk to anybody. I didn't watch TV or listen to the radio. I couldn't read anything because I couldn't hold up a book. All I did was rest and hope in God!

That's when things became clear spiritually. God visited me in quiet ways during my struggle. With no other distractions in the way, God began to speak to me, connecting the dots of my life, so to speak.

I didn't know it, but there was more testing ahead. While we were living in Kansas City where Jim was serving on a church staff, we unknowingly entered into a season of unusual spiritual warfare.

Suddenly one morning, Jim got incredibly sick. I found him delirious, hallucinating in our bedroom. I rushed him to the doctor, but for two weeks the doctor could not figure out what in the world was going on.

Almost as soon as Jim pulled through, I got slammed. We were trying to sell our home and do it ourselves. Suddenly, I became severely ill and was running temperatures that could shoot up to 104 and 105! I had been attempting to show the house to potential buyers, fighting constantly to keep it perfectly clean, and taking care of small children. After a few weeks of this frantic pace, I started to realize that there were periods of time I could not account for. My temperature was so high I was blacking out.

That was when my doctor said, "Okay, let's put you in the hospital."

After I was admitted to the hospital, things got worse. They put me in an isolation room where everyone who came to see me was required to wear a mask. The physicians started asking me the most bizarre questions. What kind of sexual relations had I had? What was my lifestyle like? Nothing was sacred, and I felt completely humiliated—stripped down to my very soul.

My lowest point came when my doctor stood at the head of my bed rattling off to himself a list of deadly diseases that I might have.

My kids had been farmed out to friends and family. They were able to visit me a few times, but the masks and robes produced such a fearful experience for them. I longed to see them and hold them, but wasn't sure what this experience was doing to them. In addition, my husband was trying to sell our home on his own.

Now here I was with this doctor who, bewildered with my symptoms, was saying, "Well now, if it's cancer we can expect to see this symptom...." He went on to catalog just about every terrible, life-threatening disease I'd ever heard of and its symptoms. Then he walked out.

There I was, lying in bed still sick as a dog. Miserable. Scared. Empty. Feeling totally alone.

I have to say that no spiritual enlightenment came my way in the long hours of that dark night. There wasn't any comforting statements like, "Yes I am with you, Ann," coming from the throne room of God. Not on that night, nor during the long days to come. I felt numb spiritually and mentally, like I had to take my head off my shoulders and not think about anything or try to process anything. I knew God promised

He would always be with me, but I couldn't feel Him, hear Him, or sense His presence. Where was He?

The Fire Bride

Through that terrible ordeal, I learned what treasure can be deposited within us as we pass through the fire when we keep our hearts open to God and to His deeper workings in our lives.

Some of us are of the mindset that God's greatest goal is to make everything easy and comfortable for us. While it's true that He wants to bless us with good things, He desires something else even more. He yearns for deep friendship with us. He longs for true intimacy!

Intimacy with God...hmm...sounds romantic, doesn't it? But our God is holy and His holiness is a consuming fire (see Deut. 4:24). How does God draw us closer to Himself? He does so by kindling a love in our hearts for Him and a deep desire to be close to Him. We become like moths that are drawn out of the darkness toward a great light—drawn by a force from beyond ourselves.

As we get closer, something else begins to happen. The fire of God begins to make us uncomfortable. The light of His holiness begins to scorch the dross and the chaff within us. We experience turmoil as we become painfully aware of our sins, shortcomings, and unworthiness to be in His beautiful, holy presence. We also become aware that we have been drawn to idolatry—false passions of the soul and flesh that have kept us trapped in worldliness.

That turmoil grows deeper and stronger until it wages a battle over our very soul. We long for Him and sense the seal of the Holy Spirit, like the engagement ring pledged as a promise of a coming wedding day (see Eph. 4:30). Yet, all of our failings, anger, jealousy, and lust are revealed before our eyes. In torment, we cry out, believing that He could not possibly love or want us as we are.

If only we could understand! Our heavenly Lover already sees and knows everything about us. And although He is aware of all our faults, He nevertheless calls us to Himself. Unfortunately, our awareness of our sin and our sense of unworthiness causes us to resist Him, holding us back from running into His arms and abandoning ourselves to Him. But there in His wonderful, gracious embrace He longs to cover all our weaknesses, needs, and sickness of soul.

We quickly discover that there is only one thing to do. In the moment of our greatest soul-agony, when we feel ourselves to be the most useless and unworthy in His eyes, we must run to Him and cry out: "Help me, my Lord and my God!"

As we rush toward Him, the wind of desperate desire fuels the flame of His passion, burning away our dross and chaff with consuming love. In this moment we begin to understand why He has allowed all the mistakes, sins, failures, and disappointments. Frances Thompson's famous poem, "The Hound of Heaven," echoes the voice of God, revealing a great mystery of His wonderful ways:

> All which I took from thee
> I did but take,
> Not for thy harms,
> But that thou might'st seek it in
> My arms.

All which thy child's mistake
Fancies as lost, I have stored for thee
at home:
Rise, clasp My hand,
and come!

We long to experience the fire of our Lover, but we're afraid to run into His arms, knowing He is a "living flame of love," as John of the Cross called Him so well. We are afraid of the process it takes to fully embrace Him and be caught up in Him forever.

So, we hang onto worldly things: passions, interests, positions, power, possessions, people—all in an attempt to anchor ourselves here on earth, and to keep from running to Him. We worry: *What will He ask of me? What will He force me to give up?* We attempt to bargain our way out of our perceived losses. *What will He let me keep?* We are blanketed with condemnation because we know we should not consider earthly "treasures" to be more valuable than Him. But we do.

Instead of being consumed by Him in the blissful joy of godly passion and the ecstasy of spiritual freedom, we are consumed by guilt instead. We know we should want Him only, but because we hold back, we begin to believe that we don't "qualify" for His love. Hopelessness begins to pull us down into discouragement and depression.

We look up in the midst of our turmoil to see a Man standing before us. As we look at Him—Jesus, the living, loving Son of God, and God Himself in the flesh—He captures us with the intense look of love in His eyes. His heart calls us so tenderly.

"Just let go of your struggle. This minute. Let it go...and come to Me!"

We begin to walk toward Him, staring into His eyes of love, and we let go of all our fear and resistance. Now, we begin to run. In our rush, the Holy Spirit breathes upon the embers of our smoldering passion, setting our hearts ablaze with love for Him.

At last, we become the Fire Bride of God.

Where she once feared the fire, to her own delighted amazement she now cries out for more. "More fire!" The intensity of heat has tried her heart, and it is becoming transformed into precious, purified gold. Her heart is pure because it is finding completion in Him and in nothing more.

Her heart will never again be polluted by other, lesser loves. For her heart is no longer hers...she has given it to Him. Her will is no longer hers, for she longs to lose it in abandonment to His. Her life and His are one.

Illuminated From Above

To finish my story, the doctors finally discovered that I had severe pneumonia and eventually were able to bring it under control. I went home to convalesce, and in time I was well again.

Despite all the turmoil and pain of that terrible ordeal, what I had needed the most I received directly from God Himself—healing for my soul. That healing was provided as I came to see God's hand in all that we had endured.

Some weeks later, after feeling my strength slowly return, I had a dream. In it, an angel came to me and hit me on the head. When he struck me my skull opened, and the light of God radiated inside me. It was 4 a.m., and I sat bolt upright in bed, charged with a supernatural energy from this encounter with God. God illuminated my understanding.

I saw clearly that God is utterly faithful to be with us at all times and through all things. Even when we allow other loves and circumstances to blind us to Him, He is still there, longing to love and be loved.

I saw something else that broke my heart. He is truly a heavenly Lover who alone has the right to claim our hearts, because no other being or thing in this universe will be as faithful as He. It is because of His unspeakable love that He deserves our full abandonment to Him.

Healing for Our Souls

Most of us think "salvation" is only about *getting saved from hell so we can go to Heaven*. But salvation is about so much more than that. Jesus opened the way for us to come into the very presence of God so that our souls, which were wounded in the fall, might be healed and restored to wholeness. We can never be whole without God. Until we rejoin ourselves to Him, we will always have a soul-wound in the place where He should be.

If we do not overcome our fear of His fire and return to His side to be made whole, we will forever be filled with that deep, empty longing for something to fill that wound. We will never fill it with the world, no matter how much we try. I have learned through turmoil, pain, and longing that God wants to heal our souls by rejoining Himself to us by the power of His Holy Spirit in us.

On this journey to the secret place with God, I am thankful that I've found spiritual "companions" to show me the way; spiritually-minded men and women who have gone through the fire themselves and come out purified. Not only purified, but they've been filled with a desire to share the grace they've received and the path they've traveled with others by means of their writings.

What I have learned about entering the secret place with God is by no means the final word on the subject. In the next chapters, we will gain more insights regarding deep and fulfilling intimacy with God from some great women of the Christian faith, including Madame Jeanne Guyon, St. Teresa of Avilla, Susanna Wesley, Fannie Crosby, Basilea Schlink, Gwen Shaw, and Beth Alves.

From these women, who have each passed through the fire, we can receive a wealth of rich insight and heavenly blessing. However, before we begin I want to offer two words of direction.

First, these teachings are to be used only as "markers." They can help us see where we might be on our own journey. The principles from their lives will not lay out a "step-by-step" list of do's and don'ts for entering into the depths of God's presence. Such approaches to spiritual growth can be canned and doomed to fail, or even worse, a form of legalism.

Second, the goal of this book is to help you sharpen your spiritual focus so that all your attention is directed toward God and God alone. Become aware of the subtle temptations you may face as you learn how to do this.

One temptation is to take our eyes off Him and turn them onto our struggles. Every time we do so, we lose sight of Him. Another is to forget His ability and refocus on our own abilities. Then, we ultimately try to change ourselves with our own puny resources. In either case, we become destined to fail.

All About Him

You see, the life we are called to live, hidden and kept in the deep love of God, is not about us at all. It is all about Him. It is all about learning that we can trust Him utterly, and abandon ourselves to Him completely. We can place all that concerns us into His care. It is all about learning to follow Him wherever He sees fit to lead us, and being used however He desires to use us.

We will begin by looking at the life and writings of Madame Guyon, whose insights about the life abandoned to our heavenly Bridegroom are among the most profound ever recorded.

Are you ready to begin this journey? Deep and daunting as it may sound, I urge you not to be afraid and don't hesitate. God is your matchless Bridegroom who wants to join Himself to you in Spirit. He has chosen you and me, and He longs to give us His Spirit, beauty, and grace, and to infuse us with His very own eternal nature.

Father, thank You that Your salvation is full and complete for both now and eternity.

Through the wisdom of those who have walked this way before us, and through Your Holy Spirit present deep within us, heal our wounds. Fill the empty longings deep inside our souls that gape like open cuts, driving us to seek comfort and satisfaction in everything but You. Open our eyes, Lord, as You opened the eyes of these great women of the faith who have gone before us. Let us see You and You alone. In Jesus' name we pray. Amen.

CHAPTER 3

THE LIFE OF JEANNE GUYON

D oes God call only a few select people to the secret place where He dwells? We may sometimes tell ourselves that, thinking God has His "favorites." But that is not the case. The truth is, God's call to the place of spiritual intimacy comes to many, but few respond. Why? I believe it's because we instinctively know there is a cost to be paid if we want to enter into deeper mysteries of God.

One person who was willing to pay the price of spiritual intimacy with God was Madame Jeanne Guyon, a French woman born into a wealthy Roman Catholic family in the 1600s. As a result of her amazing experiences in prayer she would write several books, which would become known as some the greatest writings in all of Christian history. Her books have been translated into many languages around the world, touching millions of lives.

I have found that her writings give me both courage and comfort, because I have seen in her an everyday woman with whom I can identify, nevertheless who had extraordinary experiences in God. She asked the questions I have asked: *Why did God allow that to happen in my life? Why am I so restless, and longing for more of God?*

Madame Guyon is intriguing. Not because she offers "deep answers" or "spiritual formulas," for she does not. Rather, she gives us a glimpse of the deeper work God does inside us—a work that is itself a great mystery when we become His brides of fire, fully yielded to Him.

In this journey to the secret place, Jeanne Guyon is almost a one-of-a-kind guide. Although she was an everyday woman, she went into the depths of God, which enabled her to help others find their way in the Spirit, as well.

The wisdom of this amazing Christian woman provides us with a truly unique spiritual perspective. Her words and experiences lift us up to a higher spiritual realm, the way a bird can ride the winds of an upward sweeping breeze. They allow us to soar to a higher place in spirit. Madame Guyon also gives us a godly perspective regarding the places in this spiritual journey that can wound, trouble, and throw so many of us spiritually off course. Once we gain her wise viewpoint for ourselves, we begin to see the outlines our great heavenly Lover purposes for us as He leads us on a path that is ours alone to walk with Him.

This is not just high-sounding spiritual talk. The wisdom I have gained from Madame Guyon's life and writings has helped me to understand why difficult things have happened in my life and in the lives of my children. I've been able to pass on to them godly wisdom that is guiding them in their lives through troublesome and uncertain circumstances. Consequently, I see myself growing deeper in the knowledge of God, and see myself becoming the godly mother I have longed to be. I don't know about you, but to me that kind of spiritual growth is more precious than gold!

Amazingly, it was never Madame Guyon's intent to write a book of any kind. As it happened, in the Catholic faith there were men and women known as spiritual directors, people who were responsible for the spiritual growth of anyone who was serious about faith and wanted to come under their guidance. Jeanne would go to her spiritual directors and pose all her questions. Depending upon whom she was receiving direction from at a particular time, she might or might not receive spiritual help and clarity. The main reason we have her writings at all is because her spiritual directors commanded her to write about her spiritual experiences and insights as a matter of obedience. Ironically, her questions and beliefs raised suspicion in the church and she was put in jail as a possible heretic.

Madame Guyan's profound insight came to us from a cold, dirty, stone, prison cell where she wrote in defense of the one belief upon which her faith rested—that entering in unity with God happens only as we abandon ourselves totally to Him.

She said, "...you [must become] fully convinced that it is on the nothing in man that God establishes His greatest works....He destroys that He might build. For when He is about to rear His sacred temple in us, He first totally razes that vain and pompous edifice that human art and power had erected. And from its horrible ruins, a new structure is formed, by His power only."[1]

In this one piece of writing we see the heart of Madame Guyon. Revealed is the essence of a faith that was rich, strong, alive, and unbeatable, no matter what rose up against her. So, how did she find her way into the secret place with God, the place where you and I long to go?

Beginnings

Jeanne Guyon was born prematurely on April 18, 1648, in the eighth month of her mother's pregnancy at a time when infant mortality rates were soaring. The little baby was suspended between life and death for some time, and Jeanne remained in an unhealthy state until she was almost three years old. Unfortunately, frail health would plague her all her life.

Jeanne's father was wealthy and influential and could have paid for child care provided in their home. But her mother was something of an enigma and opted to send her tiny, sick baby to a convent where Ursuline nuns would care for the baby for several months.

Perhaps her mother suffered from an unfortunate side effect of living with the emotional fallout of high numbers of infant deaths, for when Jeanne was returned to her parents, her mother's heart had cooled towards the sickly little girl and embraced Jeanne's older brother. Jeanne became neglected by her mother. In her memoirs, she recalls that her mother spent little time with her and seemed to count her of little value. She was left entirely to the care of the household servants.

On the other hand, Jeanne's father loved her dearly. When he saw his wife neglecting their daughter he arranged to send her to another convent where she might receive better care. So from the ages of four to seven, she lived at a convent of Benedictine sisters.

Despite the situation at home, Jeanne's life with the sisters would leave a lasting imprint. Living there in the convent and attending church services every day, Jeanne grew to love hearing about God, being in church, and being dressed in religious garb. Convent life planted deep seeds in Jeanne's heart of hunger for God.

In fact, she became unusually spiritually sensitive. As a little child, one night she dreamed of hell and cried out, "Oh my God, if you will have mercy on me and spare me yet a little longer I will never more offend you."[2]

Jeanne returned home briefly, but her heart would never find a home in any earthly place. Her mother, it seems, had something against the little girl from her very birth. She favored Jeanne's brother and rejected her, even ignoring Jeanne when she became ill, which was much of the time. Once she almost died of a sudden hemorrhage.

Jeanne's father sent her to another convent run by Benedictines. She was moved to yet another convent at age seven, with only brief visits home. At almost ten years of age, her father took her home again until a nun of the order of St. Dominica, a close family friend, persuaded him to permit Jeanne to live with her at her convent. When her father discovered she'd become emaciated he brought her home.

At age 11, Jeanne was sent again to the Ursulines. This time it was under the care of a half-sister who also lived with the nuns. This young woman was very nurturing, and Jeanne's spirit flourished under her care. Jeanne grew in her love and devotion to God by leaps and bounds. Later, she once again returned home.

Now all this shuttling in and out of convents, and sending children away sounds terrible to us today. But, keep in mind that it was a common practice in those days for people of means to allow their children to be brought up by monks or nuns.

For Jeanne there was some lasting benefit, because it was in the holy atmosphere of these cloisters that Jeanne felt her first touch from God. What was this deep stirring she felt inside, this sense of someone calling her? Having no instruction about a personal relationship with God through Christ, Jeanne could only feel her way through institutional Christianity. She went regularly to confession, as was the Catholic custom, and she loved prayer. Even as a child she felt a desire to suffer martyrdom. At a very young age, she and the other girls living at the convent acted out scenes in which they would take turns playing the role of martyr.

Though Jeanne would never go to a hostile foreign mission field or suffer physical martyrdom, she was destined to suffer, not only more unexplained and sudden illnesses, but martyrdom of another kind.

Soul in Turmoil

When Jeanne returned home for the last time, nothing had changed in her mother's heart; if anything, it became even harder toward the little girl. She devoted most of her attentions to Jeanne's brother, whom she allowed to be absolutely brutal toward Jeanne at times. One time he threw her from the top of a coach, badly bruising her. He often beat her. If Jeanne had something he wanted, it was taken from her and given to him. In their mother's eyes, he could do no wrong and Jeanne could do no right. As for Jeanne's care, it was mostly left to a servant girl who was allowed to beat the girl and treat her with total contempt. In fact, all the servants, if they wanted to be in good standing with her mother, would report every little "infraction."

Jeanne had to stand up under unrelenting oppression and at that time, all she had to hold onto spiritually were the written prayers in her Catholic prayer book. The kind of "talking to God" prayers that we use today was totally unheard of then. And so in moments of despair Jeanne began to cling to God, though He seemed distant.

Suddenly, at about 13 years old Jeanne transformed physically. She was quite tall for her age and was blossoming into a very pretty young woman. Suddenly, too, her mother seemed to like her more. She fussed and primped with Jeanne's hair and clothes and took her to parties and social events, and even took her traveling abroad. It became quite apparent that she was very proud of Jeanne's physical beauty.

Perhaps it was all the sudden attention, but it produced in Jeanne pride and vanity. In a way, who could blame her after being rejected for so long? However, at the same time there remained in her heart a strange tug—a sense that someone was calling to her.

At one time a cousin who was on his way to a mission in China came to visit. Something in this young man—perhaps a certain spiritual fire or a single-hearted purity—spoke deeply to Jeanne, reawakening her earlier desire for God.

She passed the next years of her life from 12 to 15 feeling torn inside. On the surface, she dressed in fine clothes, but underneath her spirit was drawn away from the fine things of the world towards an upward calling.

By reading spiritual works, such as the writings of St. Frances DeSales, Jeanne's soul deepened. Eventually, she began to spend more time with her prayer book; she was still trying to connect with that distant, elusive voice that seemed to call and then fade. The streets were full of beggars, destitute widows, and orphans; and Jeanne gave all she had to the poor. Gathering a small group of poor people together, she taught the catechism. When her parents were not at home, for her mother would have loudly disapproved, she invited the poor in to eat with her, serving them with great respect.

Alone

It was at this time that Jeanne discovered the writings of a woman known as Madame de Chantel. Never before had she heard anyone speak of the things this woman of faith talked about—especially what she called "mental prayer," what we know as *praying to God freely from the heart*. According to Madame de Chantel, it was the beginning of the way into the secret place of union with God.

Something in Jeanne's young heart leaped.

However, when Jeanne asked her confessor to teach her this kind of prayer he refused. Pray without a prayer book? He was aghast. How ridiculous! Unspiritual! Perhaps even dangerous! She should stick to the known paths. What did it matter, he said flatly, if written prayers were boring and lifeless to her? Who was she to consider other methods of prayer?

But in Jeanne's heart was a burning. She continued to fight bouts with pride and vanity. But they only drove her all the more to experience spiritual freedom. What if it were really possible to know God personally and experience Him intimately, as Madame de Chantel suggested?

She begged a community of nuns to take her in, but knowing that her father would disapprove they refused her.

So, with no one to guide her, no one she could trust to lead her on her spiritual quest, Jeanne forged ahead on her own.

Teach me how to know You, Lord! her heart cried.

She had no way of knowing where that prayer would lead.

At this same time, Jeanne's family traveled to Paris. At first, her heart was nearly overwhelmed by the whirl of social engagements, beautiful clothes, jewelry, and perfumes. Handsome suitors flocked to her door. The romantic novels Jeanne occasionally read only added to her increasing vanity. Several advantageous offers of marriage came but were rejected by her father.

Eventually, one wealthy and influential suitor did get through to Jeanne's father. One day a servant approached Jeanne with a document to sign. "Sign quickly, please! It's for your father." Taking up a quill, Jeanne inked her name...not realizing that with each letter she scratched onto the paper she was signing herself away on formal "articles of marriage." She was just 15 years old.

Two days before she was to be married, Jeanne saw her suitor for the first time. Her already turbulent young spirit sank into deep depression. Of her wedding day she would later write, "No sooner was I at the house of my new spouse than I perceived it would be for me a house of mourning."[3]

Instantly, it was apparent that Jeanne's new mother-in-law despised her. She wrote,

"At my father's house we were obliged to behave in a gentile way and to speak with propriety. All that I said was applauded. Here, they never listened to me except to contradict and find fault. If I spoke well, they said it was to give them a lesson. If any questions were started at my father's, he encouraged me to speak freely. Here, if I spoke my sentiments they said it was to enter into a dispute. They put me to silence in an abrupt and shameful manner and scolded me from morning until night.

"My mother-in-law conceived such a desire to oppose me in everything. And in order to vex me, she made me perform the most humiliating offices. Her disposition was so extraordinary...I was made the victim of her humors. All her occupation was to thwart me."[4]

Not only did this bitter old woman despise Jeanne, she turned the heart of her son, Jeanne's new husband, against her also.

"[My mother-in-law] inspired the like sentiments in her son. And so they would make people who were my inferiors take place above me."[5]

Sadly, Jeanne found no support or comfort from her own family.

"My mother, who had a high sense of honor could not endure that. When she heard [about my dishonor] from others—for I told her nothing—she chided me, thinking I did it because I didn't know how to keep my rank and had no spirit. And so I dared not tell her how it was, but I was almost ready to die with the agonies of grief and continual vexation.

"What made it worse," Jeanne writes, "was that my mother related to my mother-in-law the pains I had caused her from infancy. They then reproached me saying I was a challenging and an evil spirit. My husband made me stay all day long in my mother-in-law's room without any liberty of retiring into my own apartment. She spoke disadvantageously of me to everyone, to lessen the affection and esteem that some had entertained for me.

"She galled me with the grossest affronts before the finest company. [In this way] she found the secret of extinguishing my vivacity, and rendering me stupid. Some of my former acquaintances hardly knew me. Those who had not seen me before said, 'Is this the person famed for such abundance of wit? She can't say two words. She is a fine picture!' "[6]

Poor Jeanne, at just 16 years old she was driven to despair. Her spirit was dying, and in agony she wrote:

"I had no one to confide in who might share my affliction and assist me to bear it...I resolved to have no confidant. It was not from any natural cruelty that my husband treated me [badly]. He loved me passionately, but was ardent and hasty, and my mother-in-law continually irritated him about me."[7]

In this horrible crucible of affliction, she began to cry out to God—not in the standard formal prayers that she had been taught by the Roman Catholic church, but from the depths of her being.

"It was in a condition so deplorable, oh my God, that I began to perceive the need I had of Your assistance. This situation was perilous to me. I met with none but admirers abroad, those who flattered me to my hurt. It was to be feared, lest at such a tender age, amid all the strange domestic crosses I had to bear, I might be drawn away. But You, by Your goodness and love, gave it quite another turn.

"By these re-doubled strokes you did draw me to Yourself and by Your crosses effected what Your caresses could not effect. Not only this, You made use of my natural pride to keep me within the limits of my duty."[8]

Finding the Door

More time would pass before Jeanne made the discovery that turned all her sufferings into spiritual gold. At age 16, she had her first child, a son, and at 19, her second son was born. Both pregnancies wore her down physically, while her family continued to grind away at her spirit. Her only moments of solace were those times when she was alone crying out to God to help her.

Shortly after the birth of her second child, she met a man from the Order of St. Francis. He had lived in solitude for five years, caught up in the love of God and had just emerged from this long retreat with a kind of glow about him that was unearthly. Jeanne's father, knowing her devotion to God, arranged for her to meet with him.

There in the serene peace of monastery, away from the glare and abuse of her mother-in-law and husband, Jeanne found it difficult to contain herself. Question after question poured out from her hungry heart. The kindly brother listened with patience, not so much to her, but as though he were listening to another voice. When she finished he lifted his face to hers and stared into her eyes.

"You must accustom yourself, Madame, to seek God in your heart, and you will there find Him. For…" and he quoted the words of Jesus Christ, "…'The kingdom of God cometh not with observation…the kingdom of God is within you' " (see Lk. 17:20-21 KJV).[9]

A door to a whole new world was opened to Jeanne. The light of revelation flooded in, and she became illuminated with understanding. She realized that God was not only "out there" somewhere; the God who transcends time and space dwelled in a secret place within her. What was even more stunning was the other truth that flooded into being at the same time. She realized: If God is in me, than nothing can separate us. Nothing can come between God's love and me.

Suddenly, nothing was easier to her than prayer. Hours flew by like moments—and the joy and intensity of her devotion increased! As she put it, "The fervency of my love allowed me no intermission."[10]

Now, she was able to bear the ill treatment of her husband and mother-in-law, no matter how insulting or rigorous, silently and without turmoil. She was swept away from the cares of the world around her, having found that place inside where she could go and meet with God. Within her own soul at all times she could retreat to a secret and holy place where she could spend time with Him.

In time, Jeanne became so attuned to God's presence that she scarcely knew what she was eating. Occasionally she missed what people were saying to her, and she went for long periods without speaking.

You might think such great devotion to God would earn her the admiration of her family and of the religious community, but nothing was further from the truth.

More Opposition

Jeanne's husband became jealous of her devotion to God. Her confessor, who had previously called Jeanne a "saint," began to publicly speak against her. She had privately confided in him about her experience, and he betrayed her by spreading the word that she was under a delusion. This whole idea of meeting with God—sheer insanity!

When Jeanne's family learned about her new devotion they led the charge. She was persecuted from all sides and forbidden to pray. They went so far as to check on her every 30 minutes to interrupt her if she was in prayer. At one point, her husband refused to let her go outdoors, because she needed to be where someone could watch and control her every waking moment.

But Jeanne's understanding of prayer was far deeper than they understood. It transcended words. She now understood that true prayer is resting in the real presence of God. This revelation was so deeply embedded in her spirit that she could not stop praying. To be conscious was to be in God's living presence, with a deep abiding awareness of His strength, peace, and comfort. As a result, just the look on her face radiated the presence of God, which infuriated her family all the more.

Just when Jeanne thought she had come through the worst of the fire, she would experience the cross in ways she never could have imagined.

Shortly after the birth of Jeanne's third child, a daughter, a terrifying plague of smallpox ripped through the country of France. Her little girl and oldest son became feverish. Though Jeanne's husband wanted to take her and their younger son away to protect them, her mother-in-law refused to allow it.

To contract smallpox was to receive a virtual death sentence, and now Jeanne found herself and all three of her children stuck in this fatal trap. Fear for herself and for her children warred against her soul, threatening to tear her away from her internal place of peace with God.

Jeanne found herself in the battle of her life. When she turned her eyes and her spirit inward, there she found her heavenly King ruling all things in serene order. Nothing was beyond His control. But when she turned her attention outward to her flushed and fevered children calling piteously for water and for comfort, her mother's heart was ripped in two.

At this moment Jeanne knew that God was calling her, once and for all, to abandon the whole world and enter into the depths of love with Him alone.

Only by an act of sheer will did Jeanne make her choice. She would take her fear of loss and death to the cross and allow this part of herself to die. She knew that only in this way could she experience the peace that comes when there is nothing left to stand between God Himself...and us.

Jeanne wrote later about how she sacrificed herself to divine providence.

Almost at once, Jeanne felt the symptoms of smallpox coming on. When she told her husband he brushed it off as "just your imagination." But within hours, Jeanne was doubled over with intense stomach pain, a splitting headache, and a high fever. Still her family refused to believe she was ill. Her lungs became inflamed, and she was left gasping for breath and denied proper treatment because her mother-in-law refused to send for a doctor!

Truly, divine providence alone came to her aid. A doctor who had treated her in the past felt moved for no apparent reason to pay a call and see if Jeanne was well. She writes,

"Never was a man more surprised when he saw the condition I was in. The smallpox, which could not come out, had fallen on my nose with such force that it was quite black. He thought it was gangrened and was going to fall off. My eyes were like two coals...."[11]

The surgeon was appalled. At once, he railed at the mother-in-law for her gross negligence, only to hear her insist that he leave Jeanne alone and untreated. But while they argued, Jeanne felt only tremendous peace deep within.

"I was not alarmed....For I longed to make a sacrifice of all things and was pleased that God would avenge Himself on that face which had [in the past] betrayed me into so much faithlessness."[12]

When the doctor returned, against the mother-in-law's objections, he bled Jeanne at once. For that was the means of treating most major illnesses.

But rather than focus on her illness, Jeanne writes: "Though the smallpox came out immediately, I am more inclined to show how advantageous it is to resign oneself to God without reserve. For though in appearance He leaves us for a time, it is only to prove and exercise our faith. He never fails us when our need of Him is the more pressing."[13]

This was not the end of her terrible ordeal.

"The blackness and swelling of my nose went away, and I believe had they continued to bleed me, I would have felt better, for want of that I grew worse again. The malady fell into my eyes and inflamed them with such severe pain that I thought I should lose them both. I had violent pains for three weeks. I could not shut my eyes; they were so full of the smallpox, nor open them by reason of the pain. My throat, pallet and gums were likewise so filled with the pox that I could not swallow broth or take nourishment without suffering extremely. My whole body looked leprous. All who saw me said that they had never seen such a shocking spectacle.

"But," she continues, "as to my soul, it was kept in a contentment that cannot be expressed. The hopes of its liberty, by the loss of that beauty, which had so frequently brought me under bondage, rendered me so satisfied and so united to God, that I would not have changed my condition for that of the most happy prince in the world."[14]

The unshakable peace of her abandonment to God would sustain Jeanne through a painful loss. For though her daughter and older son survived, her younger son succumbed to the ravages of the disease.

Following her illness, Jeanne's face and body were hideously scarred. Her husband, horrified that his wife had lost her physical beauty, forced her to use an ointment "to recover my complexion and to fill up the hollows of the smallpox. I had seen wonderful effects from it upon others, and therefore at first had a mind to try them. But jealous of God's work, I would not allow it. There was a voice in my heart that said, 'If I would have had you fair, I would have left you as you were.' "[15]

Jeanne was moving deeper into her ability to trust divine providence alone. And her next move was, in a way, a declaration that she would, from now on, follow God alone. She writes that, because of her devotion to God, and against her husband's wishes, "I was obliged to lay aside every remedy, and to go into the air which made the pitting worse, to expose myself in the street when the redness of the smallpox was at its worse, in order to make my humiliation triumph where I had exalted my pride."[16]

Jeanne was moving into depths of God that few people enter though the way lies open to us all.

Total Abandonment to God

About a year later, Jeanne's daughter did die of another illness. In short order, she bore two more children.

Not long afterwards, Jeanne's husband became very ill, and it soon became apparent he was dying. Despite all the abuses he had heaped on her for years and years, as he lay on his deathbed she went to him and asked, "If there is anything I have ever done to hurt or to wound you—will you forgive me?"

Some hardness in her husband's heart must have broken, because he could only stare at her in disbelief. "No," he said. "You did me no wrong. I did not deserve you."[17]

You may well think that after her husband's death life got better for Jeanne. Instead, it got worse. For years, she continued to try to find a confessor who could understand and support her. Instead, she was assigned to spiritual leaders who disliked or distrusted her, men who were caught up in the political jockeying that often went on between the religious orders of the day. Some were even jealous of her, because wherever she went, word of her holiness and great devotion spread. People were drawn to her and tried to seek her out, though all she wanted was to live a life withdrawn from the world so she could remain caught up in the constant love of God.

It was through a "providential" meeting that Jeanne met the one man in all of France who seemed to understand her. A Barnabite Friar, Francois LaCombe, not only believed in Jeanne's spiritual wisdom, but encouraged her to write a small book, which was published in 1685 under the title, *A Short and Easy Method of Prayer*. This small work would ignite the hearts of devout men and women throughout Europe and become her most important writing, a true spiritual classic.

And it would also bring about persecution that lasted virtually for the rest of Jeanne's life. In fact, Lacombe—the one true friend she found in her lifetime—was imprisoned by the church for promoting her "heresy." He died two years after her book was published.

In 1688, at 40 years old, Jeanne also was imprisoned. It was there she was forced by spiritual directors to write more. As she wrote, she knew every word, every phrase, would be dissected by heresy hunters in the church and quite likely used against her. It was only by the intervention of Louis XIV's second wife, Madame Maintenon, that her life was spared and she was released.

Finally, Jeanne was allowed to live out the final years of her life in the solitude and peace with God she had craved throughout her entire life. On June 9, 1717, Jeanne Guyon found her way from the shackles of this earthly existence into the loving arms of her beloved heavenly Bridegroom. At long last, she was totally abandoned to the love of God.

Jeanne Guyon's Legacy

To this day, Madame Jeanne Guyon's writings are con-sidered to be among the most powerful and pure Christian writings penned by any woman in history. Great Christian leaders such as John Wesley, Count Zinzendorf, Hudson Taylor, Jessie Penn-Lewis, and Watchman Nee considered this unassuming French woman as one of their true spiritual guides.

Through her life of utter devotion, countless Christians have been taught how to find their own way into the secret place where God abides within.

Unfortunately, Madame Guyon did not have the benefit of the teachings about spiritual warfare that we have today. It is my belief that while many of the difficulties she suffered were allowed by God to train her in deeper faith, some of her sufferings were quite likely not God's will. Had she understood intercession, perhaps she could have warded off some of the attacks of the evil one. It is also my belief that she overemphasized suffering and embraced "martyrdom" in an unbalanced way, especially in her younger days. She may have even caused herself to suffer unnecessarily for the sake of God. Given the culture and times in which she was raised, we can easily overlook these imbalances for the gold that is in her writings.

Apart from these possible misunderstandings, Madame Guyon learned some vital lessons about life in the Spirit. We have much to learn from her.

First, many of us today are looking for spiritual experiences. We run here and there, to one revival after another seeking spiritual gifts and anointing. But very early in her walk with the Lord, Jeanne Guyon realized that "spiritual experience" can get in the way, and delay the work of the Holy

Spirit in us, which is destined to bring us into what she called "true union" with Him.

Writing about our need to seek nothing other than union with God, she says, "[The prayer that brings union with God] ...is far above...transports or visions, for visions are in the inferior powers of the soul and cannot produce true union. The soul must not dwell or rely upon them or be impeded by them. They are but favors and gifts, the Giver alone must be our object and aim."[18]

She warns us against loving visions, stressing how we can overemphasize them and be deceived by them. Visions are apt to create pride and vanity in the soul. Instead of attending to and loving, extolling, and praising God, we can dwell on our gifts and visions, which can lead us astray.

Second, she also warns against overemphasizing "spiritual feelings" or "ecstasies." She writes, "Ecstasies arise from a perceptible delight. They may be termed a kind of spiritual sensuality, wherein the soul, by letting it go too far by reason of the sweetness it finds in them, falls imperceptibly into decay."[19]

She even goes on to warn us about "personal Words" from God, which so many of us seek today. "And as to distinct interior words," she warns, "they too are subject to illusion. The enemy can form and counterfeit them. But the immediate Word of God has neither tone nor articulation. It is mute, silent, and unutterable."[20]

Many of her most brilliant insights come to us out of her times of loss and desperate weakness. We have already seen how she learned to press into God as a young woman with everything against her. Later in life when she was ill and could no longer visit the poor she loved so dearly, she would still insist that it was for love that God allowed even that which is most dear to your soul—your calling, gifting, or anointing—to fall away so that you might be drawn closer to Him alone.

Most importantly of all, Madame Guyon's life teaches us this wonderful truth about how we can experience intimacy with God. For she writes: "It is Jesus Christ Himself, the real and essential Word, who is in the center of the soul that is disposed for receiving Him. Never one moment ceases from His living fruitful, and divine operation."[21]

Her focus was on so loving the Lord and being so captivated by Him that she learned to bear all things with grace and humility. Because the character of Christ shone so strongly inside her, the enemy could never gain a foothold within.

May we who struggle to find God in our everyday lives learn the secret Madame Guyon knew so well. She said that "in all things, and everywhere, she found her proper center, because everywhere she found God."[22]

The hidden treasures Madame Guyon discovered were not found by her alone. She traveled a well-worn path tread upon by many others over the centuries. She was one of many women of the secret place whose lives were completely devoted and fully consecrated to knowing God.

Endnotes

1. Jeanne Guyon, *An Autobiography*, (Pittsburgh, PA: Whitaker House, 1997), 7.

2. Ibid, 12.

3. Ibid, 32.

4. Ibid, 32-33.

5. Ibid, 33.

6. Ibid, 34.

7. Ibid.

8. Ibid, 45.

9. Ibid, 47.

10. Ibid, 71-2.

11. Ibid, 72.

12. Ibid, 72-3.

13. Ibid, 74.

14. Ibid.

15. Ibid.

16. Ibid.

17. Ibid.

18. *Autobiography of Madame Guyon*, (Grand Rapids, MI: Moody Press, 1647-1717), Chapter 9.

19. Jeanne Guyon, *An Autobiography*, (Pittsburgh, PA: Whitaker House, 1997), 74.

20. Ibid.

21. Ibid.

22. Ibid.

SECTION TWO

PILGRIMS OF THE SECRET PLACE

Chapter 4

Teresa of Avila (1515–1582):
Possessed by God's Love

~

On March 28, 1515 a light flickered in a dark chapter in Spanish history. A tiny girl was born in the small, provincial Castilian town of Avila (City of Knights) in southern Spain. She was given the name Teresa de Cepeda.

It was the height of the Spanish Inquisition, in a *time* in which thousands of Jews were being slaughtered under the reign of Queen Isabella and King Ferdinand. It was also a *time* of glaring contrasts, for in the midst of such darkness it was also a season of great adventure for Spain. During this century of gold, the Spanish Armada, the conquistadors, and Christopher Columbus were discovering vast stretches of the great unknown.

Teresa of Avila was born for such a *time*. She became a beacon of light in an uncertain age, a messenger of the secret place of God's presence who modeled Christ as a place of safety, comfort, and certain refuge.

During her lifetime, her soul would often be caught away to be with God where she would be filled with visions of the Lover of her soul. She was known to call Christ "His Majesty." By the end of her life, her fellow countrymen would call her "Teresa of Jesus" and a "Doctor of the Church." But first and foremost, she simply loved God.

Childhood Years

As a young child, Teresa fiercely and passionately loved the Lord. She was the third child of her mother and the first daughter. Her father had three children by his first marriage and then nine by his second wife. So, Teresa grew up in a large family mainly of boys.[1] Her father was Don Alonso Sanchez de Cepeda, the wealthy son of a Jewish merchant from Toledo. He loved fine apparel.[2] Nevertheless, he read to his family every night about the great martyrs of Christianity.

Even as Teresa played childhood games with her little friends, her love for Jesus was never far from her mind. A favorite game was called "monks and nuns." At age seven, she convinced her brother Rodrigo to leave home with her in search of an Islamic hoard so that they might become martyrs for Christianity, thus advancing quickly into the Kingdom of Heaven.

At an early age, while other children ran and played, Teresa sought for ways to be alone with her Lord. She prayed often and turned her bedroom at home into a sanctuary where she hung a picture of Christ speaking with the Samaritan woman at the well. Teresa pleaded over and over again in prayer, "Lord, give me of that water that I may not thirst."[3]

Her mother, Doria Beatriz de Ahumada, was not yet 20 years old when Teresa was born. Beatriz spent much of her life ill, lying in bed while consuming romantic novels about a dark, handsome knight. Though her husband did not approve, Beatriz often read these romantic books to her children. By the time of Beatriz's death when Teresa was 14, it was clear these melodramas had greatly stimulated her lively imagination.

Consumed with vanity, Teresa flirted with young men and delighted in jewelry, flattery, parties, and clothing. She also developed her own romantic dramas. All these things took the place of God in her life. But all this was to change dramatically.

Life-Changing Experiences

One day, something shocking happened that put an end to everything worldly in Teresa's life. Teresa fell to the floor as if dead. Many believed that she lapsed into a coma, although little proof has been offered. Doctors found no pulse, and all attempts to revive her failed.

Thinking she was dead, the doctors left and a priest anointed her body with holy oils; prayers for the dead were recited and nuns set the body aside to stiffen before burial. Her family made funeral preparations and a grave was prepared.

Four days later, her father and her brother witnessed a supernatural fire as it hit her body. Her eyelids began blinking, her arms moved, blood rushed to her face, and she rose inexplicably. While all had been judging Teresa as dead, she was having a heavenly vision, seeing her family and communities of nuns.

By the time Teresa turned 16, she had been involved in a relationship with a young man whom her father did not approve. As a result, her father sent Teresa off to live in a strict Spanish convent-school where her social life was drastically curtailed. When Teresa entered Avila's Convent of the Incarnation, she realized that the domestic world of courtship had been closed to her, and from that moment she wanted nothing to do with the world.

Her body would need several years of convalescence while at the convent to recover from her previous paralysis and nerve-wracking pain. During this time she continued to slip in and out of consciousness. For weeks at a time, it appeared as if no life inhabited her body. To her contemporaries it seemed as though death continued to conquer this young beauty, that what lay before them was nothing more than a corpse. Yet, each time as before, Teresa would recover.

Then some time later another dramatic event took place. Teresa had a spiritual encounter with God so intense that she eventually questioned her own sanity. She saw the risen Jesus, not through physical eyes, but as in a vision through her heart. She was questioned by the nuns regarding her experience:

"How do you know it was Jesus?"

At the point of tears, she replied, "Because He told me so, over and over again."[4]

Though she had walked through the dark night of the soul with great physical pain and affliction, from this time on it seemed as though the tangible presence of Jesus was with her. She was now ruined for Heaven's sake, no longer to converse with men but with the angels.

Still, another even more intense encounter awaited Teresa of Avila some years later. In her autobiography, *The Life of Teresa of Jesus*, Teresa writes of a shining angel plunging a flaming, golden arrow into her heart. She says, "When he drew it out I thought he was carrying off with him the deepest part of me; and he left me all on fire with a great love of God."[5] She described the angel as small and very beautiful. Reflecting upon this encounter, she considered that this angel from the Lord was so illuminated that he had to be one of the very highest of the angels: the cherubim. He thrust the fiery dart into her heart several times, piercing her down to her innermost organs, leaving her with an intense love for God. She became possessed by God's love.[6]

After Teresa's death, when her heart was investigated, it appeared to have been pierced through the center as if by a dart. As late as 1872, at the request of the Prioress at Alba de Tormes, three physicians, professors of surgery, examined her heart. They found the heart still incorrupt and untouched by the ravages of death almost three hundred years later. The heart was punctured on both sides, leaving a perforation about the left and right articles, verifying what Teresa called the "transverberation" of her heart.[7]

Teresa's superiors were skeptical of her visitations, some accusing her of being influenced by satanic powers. Nevertheless, Teresa soon gained a large following as stories of her many encounters spread. At times while meditating on the Lord, she would be raptured into His presence. She would go into ecstasy, seeing the Lord Jesus while receiving the Eucharist. Many writers say that Teresa of Avila has more documented trances of Heaven and the Lord Jesus than any other person in all of church history. She was a "Christian mystic" in the truest sense.

Teresa's Life of Prayer

In her early 40's, Teresa's inner life acquired a totally fresh dimension: she was no longer in control! She speaks about her life in God in an analogy, describing it as "a new book—I mean of a new life in prayer which God has given to me."[8]

She also describes her life of prayer as a garden already planted, but one in which the plants will die unless they are tended and watered carefully. Such nurturing can be accomplished four ways. There is the laborious work of carefully drawing water from the well; secondly, there is the slightly easier method of using a waterwheel and buckets; thirdly, a stream runs through the garden, saturating the ground from beneath and lightening the gardener's load. Best of all is the fourth method: rain, the natural source of water, which entails no work at all on the part of the gardener. It comes from Heaven above.[9]

Teresa used these descriptive terms to paint a vivid picture of the stages of cultivating a life of prayer. The beginner in prayer toils, fetching water from the well. The effort is entirely his, as he attempts to fill the bucket with water and replenish the flowers of the garden. If he persists, his love for the flowers will exceed the strain of work. The privilege of seeing the arid land blossom will produce humility and endurance that will cause his soul to richly prosper.

In the second stage, the gardener uses a waterwheel and buckets. He can draw more water for the garden than before with much less effort if the long hours required do not become wearisome. This second stage can be a time of trial, when weeding and pruning is being done to the soul. Here the believer learns the *Prayer of Quiet* and the beginning of pure contemplation. Effort is still necessary, but the place of striving eases and receptivity is better understood.

The third stage of prayer is when the Lord is more active, providing water by a spring or stream running through the garden. There is now no question of turning back, the delight is too sweet; it is a glorious folly, a heavenly madness in which true wisdom is acquired.[10] Teresa said this was when Mary and Martha, action and contemplation, are in perfect harmony, though not yet entirely absorbed into God. The soul is free from worries and becomes content. God is now the gardener and the supply of water is abundant.

The last stage of the call to the secret place is where the garden is watered by rain and the gardener has nothing to do but to watch the flowers grow. This is what Madame Jeanne Guyon and many others called the *Prayer of Union*. The rain brings this union about from Heaven itself. After this type of prayer, Teresa found herself in a state of overwhelming tenderness, bathed in tears of joy. Here you know God. The sensation is of an exceeding great and sweet delight.

Love was what it was all about to Teresa; her life of prayer was the story of an intimate friendship with God. Teresa of Avila and others who have known the secret place have cherished the inner courts of the Lord. They simply followed in the paths of other forerunners who had gone before them. But, remember Mary and Martha are to be wedded together. The authentic inward journey should lead to empowered outward works.

Her Call to Reform and Renewal

While at Avila's Convent of the Incarnation, Teresa began noticing worldly habits among the women residents there. She saw that the convent still harbored gossip, slander, and vanity. Worse still, Teresa observed nuns who were more concerned about physical matters than spiritual ones. The sisters occasionally indulged in irreverence and disorder, which the house's lax rules fueled. Teresa felt that few there understood her visions or wanted to achieve that level of intimacy with God. These issues would form the basis for her lifelong effort to reform the Carmelite Order. With little support from her peers and no challenge or stimulation, Teresa began searching for a way to be of greater practical use to God. From out of her hidden life in God she bounded forth as one called to create change.

When Teresa requested that the Catholic Church permit her to live in poverty, serving the poor, a fierce controversy arose. At the time, women were considered so "radically inferior" to men, that the thought of a lone woman roaming the countryside having spiritual encounters roused the objections of more than a few religious authorities. In fact, Teresa herself held reservations about women, and was once quoted as saying, "I would not want you to be womanish in anything, nor would I want you to be like women, but like strong men. For if you do what is in your power, the Lord will make you so strong that you will astonish men." Teresa continued, "I am not at all like women,...for I have a robust spirit."[11]

In her book, *Teresa of Avila*, Carmelite nun Tessa Bielecki suggests that such statements from Teresa served two purposes: 1) to present her opinion on feminine weakness, and

2) to downplay her own femininity so as to avoid attention from the Inquisition and its scrutiny of women in the church.[12]

In 1562, when Teresa reached the age of 47, she founded a new convent of Saint Joseph's. There she spent many years teaching young women about God and her "reformed way of life."[12] She wrote two works: *The Way of Perfection* and *Meditations on the Song of Songs*. Later in April of 1567, the Father General of the Carmelite Order gave Teresa permission to found more new convents abroad. In August of the same year, she took to the road and met a man called John of the Cross while founding Medina del Campo. Teresa would eventually cofound three convents with John of the Cross, whom she would consider her spiritual advisor. Teresa planted convents at Pastrana and Toledo in 1569, Salamanca in 1570, Alba de Tormes in 1571, and several other locations over the years.

After Teresa established Alba of Tormes, religious authorities suddenly pulled her away from her tasks abroad and placed Teresa back at the Convent of the Incarnation, the place where she began her life as a nun. Despite her objections, she received the title of "prioress" for one term in the convent. Though she had spent many years there previously, Teresa noticed a severe lack of enthusiasm for her return. She was disliked and unwelcome. To combat the division and rebellion she invited her good friend John of the Cross to take the position of chaplain. Here she discovered that spiritual guides and friends are needed by all.

Friends and Guides to Teresa

Now with the combined efforts of Teresa and John of the Cross, the convent soon returned to order and harmony. Like the prophets of old, Teresa knew that at times God tends to disguise Himself as a burning bush, like the wind, and also Incarnate in man. And so it was with her relationship with John of the Cross, a man destined to become the first Carmelite friar, a mystical poet, and a "Doctor of the Church."

When Teresa's term as prioress was finally completed in Alba of Tormes, together she and John of the Cross launched out again and founded another convent, this time at Segoiva. Two were better than one, and over the years their teamwork yielded excellent results.

Then in April of 1575, Teresa met the man who would become her closest friend and advisor, Jeronimo Gracian. She called Gracian "my helper" and prayed that he would assist her in the Carmelite reform. Teresa once wrote: "I have been suffering from these Fathers of the Cloth for more than seventeen years with not a soul to help me, and it was too much for my poor strength—I did not know how to bear it any longer."[14]

Later that year, persecution as a result of her reform efforts escalated to previously unknown heights. A vengeful princess who had twice been expelled from one of Teresa's convents for outrageous behavior denounced her to the Inquisition. Betrayal followed insult as Rubeo, originally a great encourager of Teresa's work, switched sides and frowned upon her ministry. All Teresa's relationships, especially those with men, came under fire. Ambiguous rumors about sexuality slandered her chaste love for Gracian, and villains working for the Inquisition kidnapped John of the Cross and imprisoned him for nine months. The leaders of the Inquisition eventually ordered Teresa to relocate to a convent of her choosing in Castile. She lost most approval and popularity, and her life's work, her message and reformation became vulnerable. Nevertheless, her spirit continued to burn for God.

Her Writings

In 1577, between June 2 and November 29, Teresa wrote her most famous work on prayer called *The Interior Castle*, known in Spanish as *Las Moradas* (The Mansions). This is the most profound of her mystical works, a great classic based on the journey and transformation of a silkworm into a beautiful butterfly. *Las Moradas* outlines a perfect balance between the inner and the outer works of the Holy Spirit in the believer's life.

The Interior Castle was written following an extremely vivid vision, which portrayed the soul of man as on a progressive journey through a castle with many rooms. John 14:2a tells us that, "In My Father's house are many rooms." So it is in the life of each disciple. We are temples of the living God, and He has taken up royal residence within us! In allegorical language, Teresa wrote about seven rooms that one passes through on the journey to perfect union with God. She said, "The figure is used to describe the whole course of the mystical life—the soul's progress from the first mansion to the seventh and its transformation from an imperfect and sinful creature into the Bride of the Spiritual Marriage."[15]

The first mansion or room typifies the earliest and most basic stages of the Christian walk. Those at this stage know God, but still retain much of the world's influence. Numerous temptations pull at the soul, which is unable to appreciate the beauty of the castle or to find any peace with it. To progress onto the second room, one must begin to learn the lessons of humility.

To enter the second mansion requires understanding your need to respond to God's call and desiring to leave the world behind. You must gradually come nearer to the place where His Majesty dwells. You must hear His beckoning call more often, more endearing, more convicting, and more clearly than ever before. You must begin to understand that no matter how many years you live you can never hope to have a better friend than the One whose voice is calling you from the deep.

In the third mansion of the interior castle, the seeker has developed a measure of discipline and virtue in her life. The problem here arises when she begins to rely on reason, instead of love, and virtuous living, instead of God's grace. To progress on into "more Lord" one must learn the lessons of mercy in this room. Anything we receive from Him is all because of His great love, grace, and mercy.

The fourth room is captivating, for it is here that the mystical dimension or Spirit of revelation is released. The voice of the soul becomes diminished, and the waters of life rise higher. Here you enter deeper into the *Prayer of Quiet* and are consoled by God Himself. This sense of intimacy with the beloved Bridegroom entices the Bride to proceed forward into the fifth room where the metaphor of the silkworm is introduced. Here the imagery metamorphosis and the power of transformation help us to embrace the lessons of death to self and life unto God. As seekers, we now become spiritual lovers and betrothal is now the goal.

The sixth mansion is one of growing intimacy with the Lover of your soul in addition to increasing levels of tribulation, trials, and times of testing. But also in this chamber, a flood of heavenly favors of God is bestowed upon His Beloved, which intensifies the holy desire for oneness with the Lord. You become clothed in the garments of His presence with your heart beating faster with desperate love.

The seventh and final room in Teresa's extraordinary writing is that of *Spiritual Marriage* itself where complete transformation, perfect peace, and dwelling in the King's wonderful presence are realized. Here Teresa writes, "That union is like two wax candles were joined so that the light now given off is but one. Or it is as if a tiny streamlet enters the sea from which it will find no way of separating itself (nor want to) from the sea of God's immense great love."[16]

No one who makes the inward journey to the place of intimate communion with the Lord will ever be the same again. That innermost chamber of our hearts where we meet Him face-to-face is not only a sanctuary of sweet fellowship, a blissful fulfillment of holy desire, but also of glorious transformation. Like St. Teresa's silkworm, we enter that realm as humble, earthbound souls and emerge as beautiful butterflies, with our souls ready to take wing and soar.

Teresa's Legacy

We each leave a shadow in this life that will fall upon others. That is what happens when people walk in the light of God's love; the shadow of His presence is cast upon others from our lives. And so, Teresa's legacy was that the secret place became her dwelling place. All this happened despite poor health that only became increasingly fragile as she grew older. Her death surprised only a few.

An Acting Provincial (called Antonio of Jesus) sent her on an unexpected journey to Alba de Tormes. He was sexist, jealous, cold, and insensitive to Teresa's ill health and physical needs. She humbly obeyed his orders, contrary to the advice of friends. Lack of food and terrible pain marked her journey. On October 4, 1582, after finally reaching Alba de Tormes, the ailing Teresa of Jesus died from exhaustion and near starvation. She was ushered into sweet comfort and eternal heavenly bliss with a heart filled with obedience, humility, and the work of His Majesty.

Perhaps the best way to sum up the life of Teresa is in her own words written towards the end of her life. Listen to her through them, for they describe this mystical poet's great trust.

> Let nothing trouble you,
> Let nothing scare you,
> All is fleeing,
> God alone is unchanging,
> Patience,
> Everything obtains.
> Who possesses God
> Nothing wants.
> God alone suffices.[17]

Endnotes

1. Bob and Penny Lord, *Saints and Other Powerful Women of the Church* (Baton Rouge, LA: Journeys of Faith, 1989), 161.

2. Tessa Bielecki , *Teresa of Avila : An Introduction to Her Life and Writings* (Kent, England: Burns & Oates, 1994), 17.

3. Bob and Penny Lord, *Saints and Other Powerful Women of the Church* (Baton Rouge, LA: Journeys of Faith, 1989), 162.

4. Lord, 178.

5. Tessa Bielecki, *Teresa of Avila: An Introduction to Her Life and Writings* (Kent, England: Burns & Oates, 1994), 20.

6. Bob and Penny Lord, *Saints and Other Powerful Women of the Church* (Baton Rouge, LA: Journeys of Faith, 1989), 178.

7. Ibid, 179.

8. Shirley du Boulay, *Teresa of Avila: Her Story* (Ann Arbor, Michigan: Charis/Servant Publications, 1991), 38.

9. Ibid, 38.

10. Ibid, 39.

11. Tessa Bieleki, *Teresa of Avila: An Introduction to Her Life and Writings* (Kent, England: Burns & Oates, 1994), paraphrases from writings on pages 66-69.

12. Shirley du Boulay, *Teresa of Avila: Her Story* (Ann Arbor, Michigan: Charis/Servant Publications, 1991), 82.

13. Tessa Bieleki, *Teresa of Avila: An Introduction to Her Life and Writings* (Kent, England: Burns and Oates, 1994), 43.

14. Jim W. Goll, *Wasted on Jesus* (Shippensburg, PA: Destiny Image, 2001), 58.

15. Ibid, 68.

16. Bob and Penny Lord, *Saints and Other Women of the Church* (Baton Rouge, LA: Journeys of Faith, 1989), 209.

Additional Reading Material

The Interior Castle by Saint Teresa of Avila, translated and edited by E. Alison Peers, (New York, New York: Image/ Doubleday, 1989).

The Making of a Mystic by Francis L. Gross, Jr. with Toni Perior Gross, (Albany, NY: State of University of New York Press, 1993).

Majestic Is Your Name: A 40 Day Journey in the Company of Teresa of Avila by David Hazard, (Minneapolis, MN: Bethany House Publishers, 1993).

CHAPTER 5

FANNY CROSBY (1820-1915):
SONGS FROM THE SECRET PLACE

~

Fanny Crosby, the "Queen of Gospel Music" during the late nineteenth and early twentieth century, captured the heart of the secret place in thousands of hymns, which continue to rise like a sweet fragrance from the lips of God's people today.

Her hymns filled the world with music, igniting spiritual passion in rich and poor and from east and west. "Pass Me Not, O Gentle Savior" and "Saved By Grace" touched the Arab nations, Germany, and even Queen Victoria of England and the Prince and Princess of Wales.

Noted hymn writer and evangelical singer George Stebbins, said of Fanny: "There is no character in the history of the American Sunday school and evangelistic hymns so outstanding as that of Fanny Crosby, and it is quite as true that more of her hymns than of any other writer of the nineteenth century have found an abiding place in the hearts of Christians the world over. So evident is this that there is a fragrance about her very name that no other has.

"There was probably no other writer in her day who appealed more to the valid experience of the Christian life or who expressed more sympathetically the deep longings of the human heart than Fanny Crosby."[1]

In her time, Fanny Crosby was considered of equal stature with colleagues D.L. Moody and Ira Sankey. She was renowned as a preacher and lecturer and spent much of her life involved in home missions. People would line up for blocks to hear her speak.

She didn't start writing until she was in her 40's, *nevertheless* she wrote about 9,000 hymns. Her style was revolutionary for her day. Rather than following the standard, traditional form, she expressed thoughts and prayers in common words that touched the heart of worship in believers. The passion of her love for God drew the lost into the Kingdom of God.

Fanny also composed more than 1,000 poems, and played the harp and organ in concert. So many accomplishments seem incredible for any one person, but all the more when you realize that these talents were beautifully expressed through a woman who was blind from infancy!

A Flowing River of Spiritual Expression

How was such fiery passion kindled in this woman? What was her secret to discovering this river of spiritual expression—a river she surely experienced in person? Let's journey together through the milestones of Fanny Crosby's life in search of some of the keys God used to unlock the secret place within her heart!

Fanny Crosby was born into a family who was fiercely proud of their history and heritage. This rural family's heritage could be traced back to William Brewster, who sailed on the Mayflower in 1620 and was a founding father of Plymouth Plantation.

Fanny's grandfather, Sylvanus fought in the War of 1812. Sylvanus was a hardworking farmer whose land provided barely enough for his family. Mercy, the oldest daughter, married a man named John Crosby, who was nearly as old as Mercy's father Sylvanus and probably a distant cousin. John and Mercy lived with her parents to try to help out. Mercy was 20 years old when she delivered Frances Jane (Fanny) Crosby into the world on March 24, 1820.

Gayville was to be Fanny's childhood home. It was located in a rural area of Putnam County or Southeast, New York. There were 11 families who made up the Crosby clan. All who lived in the Southeast community wore the Puritan style clothing. Women's dresses were black with full skirts and white collars and cuffs. The Southeast community strictly held Calvinistic beliefs, which included the sovereignty of God's grace, divine predestination, eternal security of the believer, total depravity of mankind, and the supreme authority of the Word of God. Children learned long passages of Scripture, received just enough education to read and write, and worked the farm alongside their parents.

Damaged Vision

Fanny was about a month old when her parents noticed something was wrong with her eyes. Medical help was difficult to find in their little community; so when the family found a man who claimed to be a physician, they entrusted Fanny to his care. He placed hot poultices on the baby's inflamed eyes and told the parents the poultices would draw the infection out. The infection did leave, but Fanny's eyes were left with ugly white scars, and her vision damaged. As a result she saw little more than some light perception.

A second tragedy was about to happen to the Crosby family that same year. In November of 1820, Fanny's father, John Crosby, died from exposure. He had been working in the fields in cold, rainy weather. Twenty-one-year-old Mercy had to take work as a maidservant for a wealthy family nearby to supplement the family's income. Mercy's grandmother Eunice would care for Fanny.

Grandmother Eunice took a great interest in her granddaughter, and the two became very close during the first five years of Fanny's life. With the passage of time, it became painfully apparent Fanny would not regain her sight, and so Eunice became determined to give Fanny every advantage in training she could think of. She could not bear to see Fanny go through life treated as a helpless invalid, having to be utterly dependent on others.

Thus began Fanny Crosby's education. She sat with her family in the evenings and listened as the family read by the fireplace such works as The Iliad, The Odyssey; Paradise Lost; The Tales of Robin Hood; and the Bible. Eunice became her granddaughter's eyes, describing her surroundings to her in careful detail. Because Fanny could at times distinguish certain hues, Eunice was able to bring definition to colors.

She taught Fanny in a very holistic manner. If she used the word "bristle," for example, she would place in Fanny's hands an object to correspond to the meaning of the word. When she taught Fanny about birds, she would include the song of a particular bird, its size, shape, coloring, and the type of wings. Thus, she taught Fanny botany.

Grandmother and granddaughter would take walks together in the fall, and Eunice would describe the different types of trees and flowers. Fanny was taught by smell and touch; the leaves she knew by "handling and remembering."[2]

Then after thoroughly teaching Fanny, Eunice would test her. She would gather a pile of leaves, and one by one place them in Fanny's hands. Then she would ask, "Now, what tree is this one from?"[3] Fanny absorbed everything and developed an incredible memory and an amazing talent to communicate through description!

This was only one aspect of Fanny's education. Her grandmother taught her about God as well. Eunice had a rare gift to see God in all of creation. Creation was a mirror to her that reflected spiritual truth. In all their walks together in the woods and through the fields, Eunice brought understanding and illumination that she and Fanny were not alone, but God was walking with them! She taught Fanny that every bird, tree, and flower was designed by God to serve His plans and purposes. In this lovely path to education, Eunice taught Fanny about the loving nature of a wonderful God!

Fanny's mother, Mercy, continued laboring outside the home to earn money to support Fanny. Unfortunately, she would return home at night too tired to spend much time with her much beloved daughter. When Mercy became weighed down with weariness and worry about her daughter's future, Eunice would offer strength and support. She would come close, place her hand on Mercy's shoulder, and recite a part of a favorite hymn, or she'd quote a favorite old adage of Puritan leader Cotton Mather: "What can't be cured can be endured."

Grandmother Eunice Plants Seeds of Faith

Grandmother Eunice loved gathering the children together to read the Bible to them, explaining its stories in a language that children could understand. "The stories of the Holy Book came from her lips and entered my heart and took deep root there," said Fanny.[4]

Eunice often reminded the children of "a kind heavenly Father who sent His only son, Jesus Christ, into this world to be the Savior and friend of all mankind."[5]

Eunice was a "firm believer in prayer," and understood it was the key to a successful Christian life! She considered prayer a "close communication with her loving Savior."[6] Everything she believed about God and the importance and place of prayer was freely poured into Fanny. Grandmother spent her days teaching little Fanny how to live life by calling on God for every need, and believing in His goodness and His certain authority and power to accomplish every good work and care for every need!

Fanny learned to trust Jesus Christ, and to rest and rejoice in Him! This wise classroom of her grandmother's imparted to Fanny a place of faith, and an ability to bear her sufferings and difficulties with great grace and joy, knowing that God was always walking with her, leading and guiding, and loving her.

The little Southeast community church lacked an organ, and the congregation did not sing hymns that would be familiar to most of today's church services. Like the early Puritans, they did not believe in hymns of human composition. They used the "music" of the Psalms, which were "dictated" from God to David, and chanted them without any musical accompaniment. The only person in the church with a copy of the hymn was a deacon who stood at the podium or desk. He would recite a line of the psalm and then the congregation would repeat it after him until they had recited the entire psalm.

This form of worship created a hunger in Fanny's heart for greater expression. To her it was lifeless. Fanny loved singing and fed her soul listening to the music of nature. She truly wanted to experience life and did not consider herself as different from other children, except when someone would make a comment to that effect. She was a happy and contented child. Eunice and Mercy would let Fanny play outside at night with the other children of the town within the vicinity of their house. For Fanny, playing at night was not anything unusual.

When Fanny was five years old, Mercy took her to the Columbia University School of Medicine, in New York City, to be examined by Dr. Valentine Mott, considered one of the top surgeons in the United States. He confirmed Mercy's worst fears, that the "doctor" who had treated Fanny Jane's eyes had done irreparable damage. Mercy comforted her daughter by assuring her that God had a special plan and purpose for

Fanny's life! On the way home, Fanny had an experience with God.

"As I sat there on the deck amid the glories of the departing day, the low murmur of the waves soothed my soul into a delightful peace. Their music was translated into tones that were like a human voice...."[7] The experience touched Fanny deeply.

Mercy landed a new housekeeping job, requiring mother and daughter to move six miles away from their present home. Everything changed for Fanny, because Mercy was much more apt to freely apply the rod for correction, in contrast to Eunice's gentler approach. Nevertheless, Mercy truly loved her daughter and cared for her needs as best she could. Fanny learned to climb trees "like a squirrel," rode horseback, and climbed stone walls.

Eunice visited often and continued teaching Fanny everything she could. Fanny truly learned that as a blind person she could still do almost anything a sighted person could do. Still, she went through times of discouragement when she asked God "whether, in all His great world, he had not some little place for me."

In response, Fanny heard Him reply, "Do not be discouraged, little girl. You shall someday be happy and useful, even in your blindness.[8]

Fanny's First Poem

When she was eight years old, she composed her first work, which reads as follows:

Oh, what a happy child I am,
Although I cannot see!

94

I am resolved that in this world
Contented I will be!
How many blessings I enjoy
That other people don't!
So weep or sigh because I'm blind.
I cannot—nor I won't.

A year later, Mercy and Fanny moved to Ridgefield, Connecticut, where Fanny was destined to receive another installment in her training. Mrs. Hawley, a landlady who cared for Fanny while Mercy was at work, made it a goal for Fanny to memorize the entire Bible! Fanny would learn a few chapters each week. She mastered Genesis, Exodus, Leviticus, Numbers, and the four Gospels by the end of the year. Within two years, she had also memorized many of the Psalms, all of Proverbs, Ruth, and the Song of Solomon! She carried on this task throughout the rest of her life. Gradually, she eliminated the need for someone to read the Bible to her; she had ingested it into her being!

In addition, Mrs. Hawley also included selections from secular works for Fanny to memorize, including various poems of the day.

Fanny was introduced to the hymns of Charles Wesley and Isaac Watts, when she would occasionally visit a Methodist church. She loved their majestic sound!

As Fanny reached adolescence, she became increasingly troubled over her handicap at times. She began competing with her friends, trying to prove what a blind person could do. She also spent many hours thinking, pouring over the Scriptures. She felt more and more alone. Finally one night, she was able to talk to her grandmother about this ache in her heart. They prayed together, and Fanny remembered the night, "was beautiful. I crept toward the window, and through the branches of a giant oak that stood just outside, the soft moonlight fell upon my head like the benediction of an angel, while I knelt there and repeated over and over these simple words: 'Dear Lord, please show me how I can learn like other children.' "[9] She felt an immediate release from the anxiety that had weighed down upon her. It was "changed to the sweet consciousness that my prayer would be answered in due time."[10]

"By God's Grace I Will"

On a summer evening in 1831, Fanny and her grandmother would be together one last time. Eunice became very ill and knew she was about to die. She told Fanny, "Grandma's going home." In her soft, frail voice she asked, "Tell me, my darling, will you meet Grandma in our Father's house on high?"

Fanny responded, "By the grace of God, I will." Eunice drew Fanny to herself one last time, and they prayed their last prayer together. Eunice Crosby died a short time later, at the age of 53.[11]

These early years laid the foundation stones of preparation in Fanny's life. She would discover a wonderful singing talent, learn to play the guitar, become an accomplished horsewoman, and develop a reputation as a storyteller. But where she really shone was in her poetry. She was about to explode into fulfillment of God's purpose for her life!

A age 14, a wonderful door of opportunity opened. Fanny enrolled in the New York Institution for the Blind, where she would spend 20 years of her life. She was educated in English grammar, science, music, history, philosophy, astronomy, and political economy; and she learned Braille, although she struggled with it. Her fingertips had been callused from playing guitar, which made it difficult to feel the raised letters. She also memorized the complete text of Brown's Grammar.

Fanny's enthusiasm for poetry continued to grow, but her teachers at the Institution felt she was letting this ability puff up her head. One of her instructors reprimanded her, saying, "not to think too much about rhymes and the praises that come from them." At first she was hurt, but then, "through tears, she composed herself, threw her arms around his neck, and kissed his forehead. 'You have talked to me as my father would have if he were living. And I thank you for it.' "[12]

She continued to grow in her education and various talents and skills, and at the age 20 was considered the institution's most promising student. She showed such promise in her poetic talent that she was given a poetic composition teacher named Hamilton Murray. Mr. Murray played an invaluable role in her training. He gave her long poems to memorize, and taught her the use of rhyme, rhythm, and meter, as well as encouraged her to imitate well-known poets.

Fanny consumed all these components of poetry and learned to compose quickly. This training was the foundation stone that would later enable her to compose as many as 12 poems a day. She became known as "the blind poetess."

Visitors to the institute would be shown the works of its brightest students. President John Tyler, New York Governor

William Henry Seward, and Count Bertrand, Napoleon's field marshal, were just a few who visited. During her time with the school, first as student, then later as instructor, Fanny contributed to various New York poetry columns and published four books of poetry. She knew her recognition as "the blind poetess" was gaining much needed attention to the institute and the needs of the blind, and was delighted to serve in this way. She was so grateful to the institute and had no aspirations of a greater personal platform.

Would She Be Ready?

In the year 1848, cholera broke out and Fanny contracted the disease. She recovered, but her close brush with death made her think about dying. Would she be ready to meet God? She had believed in God and His goodness but had never experienced conversion. During this time of seeking and soul-searching, Fanny dreamed she visited a dying man. The man asked her if she would meet him in Heaven after their deaths. She responded in the dream that by God's help, she would—the same response she had given her grandmother. The dream ended as the man said, "Remember, you promised a dying man!"

The experience drew Fanny to a deeper place of seeking God. She attended revival meetings and went to the altar twice, feeling nothing had changed. However, the third time she went to the altar, something happened!

"During the fifth verse of 'Alas and Did My Savior Bleed?' Fanny prayed, 'Here Lord, I give myself away. 'Tis all that I can do.' Suddenly Fanny felt 'my very soul was flooded with celestial light.' She jumped to her feet, shouting, 'Hallelujah! Hallelujah!' She said, 'For the first time I realized that

I had been trying to hold the world in one hand and the Lord in the other.' "[13]

Fanny's life was dramatically changed! She called it her "November experience." From that point on, her life was totally dedicated to God. A desire to do His will alone consumed her, and all other desires fell away into the dust. It is from this experience that many of her later hymns were birthed. One unpublished poem, called, "Valley of Silence," explains more than any other of Fanny's writings, her mystical experience of November 20, 1850. She wrote this poem two months before she died.

> I walk down the Valley of Silence,
> Down the dim, voiceless valley alone,
> And I hear not the fall of a footstep
> Around me, save God's and my own;
> And the hush of my heart is as holy
> As hours when angels have flown.
> Long ago I was weary of voices
> Whose music my heart could not win,
> Long ago I was weary of noises
> That fretted my soul with their din;
> Long ago I was weary with places,
> When I met but the human and sin.
> Do you ask what I found in this Valley?
> 'Tis my trysting place with the Divine,
> For I fell at the feet of the Holy,
> And above me a voice said, "Be Mine."
> And there rose from the depth of my spirit,
> The echo, "My heart shall be Thine."
> Do you ask how I live in this Valley?

I weep and I dream and I pray;
But my tears are so sweet as the dewdrops
That fall from the roses in May,
And my prayer, like a perfume from censers,
Ascendeth to God night and day.

Called to the Secret Place

The sweetness and nearness of God is so evident in this poem. Fanny surely knew the call to the secret place. There are so many other events in Fanny's life that have not been touched upon. She moved forward with her life, married, and had a child who sadly died in infancy. She met presidents and befriended influential people. Living during a time when a national Sunday school movement was sweeping the nation, when mission societies were proliferating, and when a revival called the Second Great Awakening was shaking America, Fanny Crosby found plenty of opportunity to put her well-honed talent and skill to work.

Gold Poured Out to the World

God blessed Fanny by connecting her with songwriters who would open doors to the hearts of the masses. Fanny's years of preparation in difficulty, poverty, and hardship had refined her heart into gold that was now ready to be poured out into the world.

How did she find that place in God? From which treasures of her life experiences can we glean and learn? Let's now examine some of these treasures, take them into our own hearts, and deeply cherish them. For the treasures of the Lord are always to be shared and given away, to be blessed and multiplied to the lives of those who live for God with holy desperation.

For a child to have a mentor is truly God's gift, and Fanny had a wonderful mentor in her grandmother Eunice. Eunice taught her to believe in the goodness and faithfulness of God. Believing is the antidote to bitterness, resentment, and fear. Fanny literally was led by the hand and walked through pastures, woods, and valleys as she was taught of God's faithfulness in creation. Grandmother Eunice taught young Fanny to look for and find God in every place and every situation. He is there, but we have to be taught to expect to find Him!

The Bible tells us to renew our minds by meditating on the Scripture. Finding the secret place also requires discovering markers to point the way. Never forget that reading and meditating on God's Word permits our Father to speak to us about what's important to Him. He longs to share His secrets. The power, illumination, and transformation available through the Word are beyond description!

Embracing Jesus

Fanny associated with the poor in spirit, slum dwellers, alcoholics, and prisoners. She gave herself to a life of simplicity, giving away money and aid to those in need. She knew God's heart for the poor and needy, and in embracing them she embraced Him. One of the keys to the secret place is having a tender place in our hearts for the alien, the orphan, and the widow.

Fanny did not equate giftedness with godliness. She freely gave away the gift that God deposited within her. She wrote under at least 204 pen names, and she wrote verses for friends who published them with their own melodies. No one actually knows just how many hymns and poems she wrote. Do you think she really cared?

Fanny knew the power of distraction and would purpose to have time alone with God in the long night watches. She daily carved a place to be alone with Him, even though it meant sleepless nights. He was her rest and peace!

By employing all her energies to realize the full maturity and effectiveness of her gifting, Fanny learned how to apply herself. She harnessed the strength of her mind to the Spirit of God enabling her mind to become an effectual tool. She brought her mind, her mental ability into the secret place.

In addition, Fanny learned to embrace concern and even criticism from others, allowing them to work true humility into her life! She established a lifestyle of selflessness, not giving room in her heart to pride. She learned to receive from God and others, whether in gentleness or in conflict, and ask God to make her heart right within her.

The grace of God is boundless, and His Truth is unending. We are on a journey in which we never "arrive" until the day we enter Heaven's doors. Fanny Crosby is there now, beholding His face. God's gift through her is still giving life and hope to countless people. The warmth of its radiant glow continues to light the way to that secret place in God!

> Savior, more than life to me,
> I am clinging, clinging close to Thee;
> Let Thy precious blood applied
> Keep me ever near Thy side.

Every day, every hour,
Let me feel Thy cleansing power;
May Thy tender love to me
Bind me closer, closer, Lord to Thee.

Endnotes

1. Bonnie C. Harvey, *Fanny Crosby, Woman of Faith*, (Minneapolis MN: Bethany House Publishers, 1999) 11.

2. Ibid. 20.

3. Ibid. 20.

4. Ibid. 21-22.

5. Ibid. 22.

6. Ibid. 26.

7. Ibid. 28.

8. Ibid. 32.

9. Ibid. 32.

10. Ibid. 33.

11. Ibid. 39.

12. Ibid. 54.

13. Ibid. 55.

Bibliography

Fanny Crosby, Woman of Faith, by Bonnie C. Harvey, Bethany House Publishers, Minneapolis MN, copyright 1999.

Fanny Crosby, The Hymn Writer, Heroes of the Faith, by Bernard Ruffin, Barbour Publishing, Inc, Uhrichsville, OH, copyright MCMXCV.

"Fanny Crosby, She Blesses Us Still", Decision Magazine, March 1990, pages 23-24, by Leslie K. Tarr

Handbook to the Baptist Hymnal, Fanny Jane Crosby, Convention Press, Nashville, TN, copyright 1992.

Fanny Crosby's Story of Ninety-Four Years, Retold by S. Trevena Jackson, Distributed by The Blakiston Company, Philadelphia & Fleming H. Revell Company, New York and London.

CHAPTER 6

SUSANNA WESLEY (1669—1742):
THE MOTHER OF REVIVAL

—◝◞—

M ore than 2000 Puritan pastors were forced to stop prac-
ticing their faith under the reign of English Royalist
King Charles II. Nevertheless, Puritan pastor Dr. Samuel Annesley flatly refused. The consequences of opposing the king
of England were harsh. Samuel was evicted from his clerical
position, harassed and forced to undergo hardship at the
hands of the authorities. Still, he never wavered from his
courageous convictions.

Born into this religiously tumultuous time was Samuel's
impressionable young daughter Susanna.

England had become embattled in a religious civil war.
Royalists fought for King Charles I and the Church of England against the Parliamentarians who sided with the Puritans, a religious sect that had separated from the Church of
England. The Parliamentarians emerged as the victors, but a
few years later, the Royalist army with King Charles II re-
gained power. Consequently, in 1662 legislation was passed

forcing all ministers to conform to the practices and beliefs of the Church of England. This legislation was called the Act of Uniformity. When 2000 pastors refused to conform, the Great Ejection followed.

Ten years later, King Charles II recanted somewhat and decided to permit religious freedom to a certain extent. Samuel then started a new ministry, reaching out to the poor, the fatherless, and the widows in London. All these events were to imprint on Susanna's heart the basic principles of the Christian religion.

A Mother of Superior Understanding

Susanna Annesley's life began on January 20, 1669. She was born in London, the 25th child of Dr. and Mrs. Annesley. Although 25 children were born, records show only seven surviving to maturity. The Annesleys were deeply devout Puritans and wholeheartedly committed to raising their children to fear the Lord. Although Susanna's mother's name is not known, historical research reveals that she was deeply loved by her husband, who expressed great desire to be buried in her grave. She appears to have been a woman of superior understanding and earnest, consistent piety. She was devoted to promoting the religious welfare of all her children.

Samuel found great fulfillment in educating people in the ways of the Lord. He could not remember a time when he did not know the Lord. At five years of age, he began reading 20 chapters of the Bible every day.

He graduated from Oxford University in 1644, and became a pastor of a church in the county of Kent. Although he endured threats on his life, the people of Kent experienced

God's grace upon their lives through his ministry. Later, he moved the family to London.

Susanna grew into a very accomplished young lady. She pursued the study of many subjects, including other religious beliefs and the political views of the day. Her parents provided her with a thorough knowledge of the Bible and a well-rounded education, probably through her mother's teachings, as it was uncommon for girls to be formally educated in those days.

Susanna excelled, having amazing mental abilities. She studied logic, metaphysics, philosophy, and theology. She also became proficient in French and in English grammar. Digging deeply into the religious controversy that engulfed England at the time, Susanna entered into debates with her father and his guests as they discussed these difficult matters. Before 13 years old, Susanna had studied the entire controversy between the Church of England and the Dissenters. She gained the respect of her elders for her opinions and insights.

Raised in a family considered to be radical in its beliefs and uncompromising in its principles, Susanna was given a solid foundation that would serve her well in the times to come.

Susanna met her future husband, whose name was Samuel like her father's, in her parent's home. He was often a guest of her father and participated in the discussions in which Susanna took part. Samuel Wesley also came from a long family line of nonconformists, and his father was a minister who had been affected by the Great Ejection of 1662.

Samuel Wesley's father had held meetings in secret and was imprisoned four times. He died at the age of 42 when

Samuel was quite young, and young Samuel Wesley was sent to various academies in London. During these years, he became convinced that he should join the established Church of England, and so he turned away from his Puritan roots.

At the time he made this decision, he and Susanna were probably discussing these matters together. They both, separately but simultaneously, made the same decision to join the Church of England. They were married between November 1688 and the spring of 1689.

Love and Commitment

Samuel and Susanna had very different temperaments. Samuel was outgoing and loved laughing and telling jokes. Unfortunately, he was also a poor money manager, which would create great difficulty for the couple in the years to come. Susanna was introverted, quiet, and gave little time to humor. She was very methodical in her approach to life, and though she was very passionate she kept her emotions in check. Despite their strong personalities and great differences, Susanna and Samuel loved each other very much. Samuel lavished constant praise and respect upon Susanna. In the years ahead, their love and commitment for each other would be greatly tested.

Only two years after their marriage, children began to come quickly into the world. Their first son, Samuel, was born February 10, 1690. Then came Susanna in 1691. Emilia followed in 1692. At this time, Susanna's body became inflicted with rheumatism, as well as the physical strain of her pregnancies being so close together. In 1694, little Susanna died, which must have been terribly painful for Susanna and Samuel. Twin boys were born at the end of 1694, named Annesley and

Jedediah, but both died after only one month. In 1695, Sukey was born. Her legal name was Susanna, after her deceased sister. Child number seven came along in 1696 named Mary, and then Hetty came in 1697.

At this time, the burgeoning family received a new ministerial assignment. It promised to bring an increase in salary, and the rectory was larger and more suitable for their growing family, or so they thought. Actually, it turned out to be a hardship. The buildings were in great need of repair. Samuel's debts began to grow, and children were being added to their family at the rate of at least one per year. This period of time brought them to the brink of marital crisis! A second set of twins were born in 1701, a boy and a girl. The infants must have died shortly after their birth, because they never were named. Then baby Anne was born late in 1702.

In 1702, financial difficulty increased, which brought Samuel more distress than ever.

Their marital differences climaxed with Samuel leaving Susanna and the children for a period of time. As Samuel was on his way to London, he learned that their house had caught fire. He returned home immediately, and the realization that he nearly lost his entire family brought him to his senses. He remained at home, repaired the house, and resumed his clerical duties. He and Susanna made a fresh start, forgiving each other and putting the whole difficult time behind them.

John Wesley came along in 1703, followed by his brother Charles in 1705. Both John and Charles entered the world in a very fragile state, but as time passed their health improved.

The Wesleys endured much hatred and evil acts against them by the people from the surrounding area. Because there was much religious controversy in those days with a large number of the general population not wanting to have anything to do with God or the church, many people vented their feelings. As a result, the Wesleys were threatened, their fields were set ablaze, their cattle were attacked, and the children were often put to bed under a hail of gunfire near their home at night. Of course the children were afraid and rarely ever went outside. During this time, Susanna and Samuel lost another child.

Adding to the family's difficulty, a creditor had Samuel imprisoned for a debt of 30 pounds, forcing Susanna and the children to live on the earnings from their tiny dairy, and the scant amount of money she had. Although they suffered through terribly sorrowful and hurtful times, Samuel was impressed by his wife's resilient and steadfast spirit!

God Spared Their Son

A terrible fire occurred in the dead of winter in February 1709, probably set by mean-spirited local townspeople. Not only did it ravage all their possessions, it almost took little John Wesley's life. He was saved by a neighbor who rescued him from the second story. Susanna lost all her books, her teaching papers, and her family treasures. Nevertheless, she was grateful to God for sparing her son's life.

After the fire, Samuel and Susanna, along with two-year-old Charles, went to live with one of their few friends. Their 19th and final child, Kezzy, was born at this time. The rest of the children were sent to live in various homes until Susanna and Samuel could reestablish the Wesley household. Susanna was learning the difficult lesson of trusting God completely, especially in the face of disaster and years of real physical and emotional need. She did not allow herself to plummet into despair but was strengthened with her sense of abandonment to God, believing that she was the Lord's. He could do with her life as He pleased.

Samuel completed repairs on their home, this time with fire-resistant bricks, and the Wesley family was reunited. Still, the neighboring people clung to their harsh judgments against them and continued to desire them harm. Nevertheless, God was about to change the climate!

Although 1712 began in hardship, Samuel Wesley felt it necessary to attend a religious convocation in London. Besides bringing even more financial stress upon the family with travel expenses and having to pay a curate to care for his parish, it also meant he would be absent from his family for months on end.

While he was away, five of the children came down with smallpox. In addition, the temporary curate began working to undermine Samuel's position, purposely preaching about the evils of indebtedness, knowing full well that it was an unresolved issue in Samuel Wesley's life. Susanna was in a difficult place. The church lacked genuine spiritual guidance, her husband was being openly disrespected, and she disagreed with this man's stance of having only one church service on Sunday.

With her children's welfare in mind, Susanna decided to hold meetings in their kitchen on Sunday evenings. She included not only her children but the servants also. They sang psalms, read prayers and she preached a sermon taken from Samuel's library. Word spread into the community concerning these meetings, and soon there were 30 to 40 people in attendance.

Susanna began earnestly meeting with each of her children individually to determine the condition of their souls and their commitment to God. She searched for the most impressive sermons she could find and read them to her gathering of hungry hearts. Soon, the attendance grew to standing room only—about two hundred people!

When Susanna wrote a letter to Samuel informing him about the meetings, Samuel responded expressing many concerns. He was unsure they should continue. Susanna wrote back in a very straightforward manner, going head-to-head with each one of his arguments with clarity and humility. After receiving her response, Samuel gave his approval. The meetings continued, and both the family and community experienced the grace of God in a beautiful way.

Stop the Meetings!

Susanna's success unleashed furious anger and jealousy from the curate, Mr. Inman. He wrote a letter to Samuel, accusing Susanna of holding illegal religious meetings. Afraid her gatherings would bring disapproval from the church and ruin his future ministerial career, Samuel changed his stance and asked Susanna to stop the meetings!

Susanna's reply to this latest challenge is worthy of quoting, at least in part. The following statements are taken from her letter to Samuel:

> I shall not inquire how it was possible that you should be prevailed on by the senseless clamors of two or three of the worst of your parish, to condemn what you so lately approved...It is plain in fact that this one thing has brought more people to

church that ever anything did in so short a time. We used not to have above twenty to twenty-five at evening service, whereas we have now between two and three hundred; which are more than ever came before to hear Inman in the morning....Now, I beseech you, weigh all these things in an impartial balance: on the one side, the honor of almighty God, the doing much good to many souls, and the friendship of the best among whom we live; on the other, the senseless objections of a few scandalous persons...and when you have duly considered all things, let me have your positive determination...If you do, after all, think fit to dissolve this assembly, do not tell me that you desire me to do it, for that will not satisfy my conscience; but send me your positive command, in such full and express terms as may absolve me from all guilt and punishment, for neglecting this opportunity of doing good, when you and I shall appear before the great and awful tribunal of our LORD JESUS CHRIST.[1]

What fire was burning in her soul! There is no record of Samuel writing back and demanding that Susanna stop the meetings. They continued until he returned home.

Samuel reaped great benefit from his wife's efforts. His children were being spiritually nurtured. His parish was growing considerably in attendance and in the grace of God. His neighbors, who before had fired their guns off in front of his home terrorizing the children, and who probably had been responsible for setting their home on fire, were now supporting them for the first time. His children felt secure enough to now play freely outside. The most important benefit of all was that the form and structure of Susanna's meetings would eventually make up the basis for the entire Methodist movement!

All this was accomplished by a woman's commitment to nurturing in her children a love for God. God lit a fire in Susanna's soul that would eventually ignite many souls around the world! She discovered a balance in walking within the boundaries of understandings of her time period, and yet daring to step out and do something for God's sake! She honored her husband and submitted herself to him, but she was confident enough to be different, to do what had never been done before in the midst of great criticism.

An Innovator and Educator

Susanna was an innovator in education! She believed in a good education, including religious training for both boys and girls equally, and she was convinced that the only way she could be sure it would happen was to do it herself! She actually developed extensive teaching manuals, including three theological manuals. The first discussed the order and design of creation and how it testified to God's existence. The second manual dealt with the great doctrines of the Christian faith using the Apostle's Creed. The third manual expounded upon the Ten Commandments, teaching the major tenants of divine moral law. She also wrote many theologically instructive letters to her children.

Susanna believed in ordering her children's daily schedule. She taught her children to honor their parents, and she believed that bringing a child's will into subjection to the parents and to God was the key to nurturing their spirits. All of Susanna's teachings were constantly undergirded by her love and devotion. The Wesley children excelled under her love and instruction, and they learned to truly respect and love their mother all their days.

Susanna cared for nothing more on the earth than the salvation of her children's souls! Her writings were filled with understanding and instruction. She wrote concerning the sin of the will, the sin of the imagination, the sin of the memory, the sin of the passions of the soul. She said that "sin is the greatest contradiction imaginable to his most holy nature."[2] About God, she wrote, His "infinite purity, absolutely separated from all moral imperfection."[3] "He is goodness, and his most holy will cannot swerve or decline from what is so. He always wills what is absolutely best; nor can he possibly be deceived or deceive anyone."[4] "But the infinite goodness of God, who delights that his mercy should triumph over justice, though he provided no remedy for the fallen angels, yet man being a more simple kind of creature, who perhaps did not sin so maliciously against so much knowledge as those apostate spirits did, he would not subject the whole race of mankind to be ruined and destroyed by the fraud and subtlety of Satan; but he gave us help by one who was mighty, that is able and willing to save to the uttermost all such as shall come to God through him."[5]

By powerfully impacting her children, Susanna touched the entire world. Her message of devotion to God and hunger to see lost souls come to God lived on through her children. John and Charles testified often of her great influence. All of them looked to her for wise counsel throughout their lives.

Susanna's message was prepared and ready to be released into a society whose time was ripe for harvest. In eighteenth-century England, religious conviction had become a rare commodity. The country was replete with gambling and drinking. Cheap gin raised the death rate dramatically. Reason was exalted above the Bible, and Christianity was reduced to only a code of ethics. Lost was the understanding that sin must be forgiven and cleansed, and gone were beliefs in a miracle-working God and God who also became man.

Passing Down the Seed of Spiritual Desire

The precious seeds Susanna had so tirelessly and diligently sowed and watered into the lives of her children were beginning to bear fruit in John and Charles Wesley! These young men grew up hungry for God.

In 1728, Charles experienced an awakening in the Spirit while he and John were attending Oxford University. He began praying and ministering to the sick and needy, and eventually formed what was called the Holy Club, later known as the Methodist Society. John joined the group and became a leader within this new movement.

John and Susanna exchanged many letters discussing doctrinal issues. She helped him formulate the foundation stones for the Methodism. John was convinced that the gospel message could transform society! He modeled what he had experienced in those Sunday evening meetings led by his mother. He witnessed the fruit of his mother's devotion to God and her preaching and continued on with the concept. These meetings, started in a kitchen while her husband was away, became the hallmark of the Methodist movement. They became known as lay preaching, and Susanna was the first to voice her support.

On May 21, 1738, Charles attended a meeting with a Moravian Society, a fiery evangelistic group that preached justification by faith alone. This meeting was not about mere doctrine but was a life-changing experience.[6] During this meeting, God touched Charles and he received an assurance of his salvation.

Three days later, in what has become known as his Aldersgate Street experience, John had a similar encounter with the same Moravian society. His now famous words were spoken: "I felt my heart strangely warmed. I felt I did trust in Christ, Christ alone for salvation; and an assurance was given me that he had taken away my sins, even mine, and saved me from the law of sin and death."[7]

John had been ordained as a minister in the Church of England but was expelled because of these fanatic ideas. So, he took to the streets and open fields, preaching wherever people would listen. As a result, many people came to Christ. He took a stand against drinking and slavery and began changing the climate of the nation! He opened the first free medical dispensary in 1746 and spent much of his time visiting the sick, ministering to the poor, and preaching to the masses. John's heart became so large that he felt called to the world and claimed it as his parish.

Charles became known as one of the greatest hymn writers in the world, having written the words to over 6,000 hymns. He clearly articulated true, theologically sound hymns, and most of those songs continue to be vibrantly sung today. His inspiring music has traveled around the world!

John and Charles Wesley were the figureheads in a revival that transformed Britain and America and birthed the

Methodist movement. Tens of thousands of churches have sprung up around the world, and millions have been brought into the saving grace of Jesus Christ. Much needed social reform also grew out of this awakening!

You Must Let God Impact You!

Like Susanna, you can dramatically impact the world by impacting your children. But first, you must let God impact you!

Susanna's personal life was filled with many difficulties. Her husband, Samuel, suffered a stroke at the age 64 in 1726. He still owed much money and had no savings. On April 25, 1735, Samuel Wesley died. Susanna moved out of the family home and lived first with her daughter Emilia for a year, then a year with Samuel, then with daughter Martha for two years. After her son Samuel's sudden death in 1739, she went to live with John in London and lived the rest of her days in his little apartment. She fully participated in her son's ministry. It was while she was living with John that Susanna had another experience with God. She was attending a communion service, when she like John and Charles experienced a deep, inner sense of knowing that her sins truly were forgiven.

Susanna had faithfully loved God and served Him every way she knew how. She dogmatically believed one needed to regularly search the heart and confess sin. She also believed in developing a thoroughly biblical foundation for one's life, and she prayed ceaselessly for the salvation of her children's souls. She was a person, in process, just as we are. She did not receive a revelation of the assurance of salvation until later in life, but that did not stop her from pursuing all these other wonderfully valuable aspects of her life of faith and developing her secret place in God!

Susanna experienced the loss of yet one more child before her soul would pass on to Heaven. On March 9, 1741, Kezia died at 30 years of age. Less than a year later in July 1742, Susanna herself was at death's doorstep. Aware of her soon passing and fully assured of her salvation, she was at peace. She asked her children to sing a psalm of praise to God at her funeral.

The following words were inscribed in the tombstone of this great lover of God:

> Here lies the body of Mrs. Susanna Wesley,
> the youngest and last surviving daughter
> of Dr. Samuel Annesley.
> In sure and steadfast hope to rise
> And claim her mansion in the skies,
> A Christian here her flesh laid down,
> The cross exchanging for a crown.
> True daughter of affliction, she,
> Inured to pain and misery,
> Mourn'd a long night of griefs and fears,
> A legal night of seventy years:
> The Father then reveal'd his son,
> Him in the broken bread made known;
> She knew and felt her sins forgiven,
> And found the earnest of heaven.
> Meet for the fellowship above,
> She heard the call, "Arise my love."
> "I come," her dying looks replied,
> And lamblike, as her Lord, she died.[8]

Years later, her tombstone was changed to reflect her faithfulness to her husband, and respect for her sons, John and Charles.

Here lies the body of
MRS. SUSANNA WESLEY,
Widow of the Rev. Samuel Wesley, M.A.
(late Rector of Epworth, in Lincolnshire,)
who died July 23, 1742,
aged 73 years.
She was the youngest daughter of the
Rev. Samuel Annesley, D.D.
Ejected by the Act of Uniformity
From the Rectory of St. Giles's,
Cripplegate, August 24, 1662.
She was the mother of nineteen children,
Of whom the most eminent were the
REV. JOHN WESLEY AND CHARLES WESLEY;
The former of whom was under God the
Founder of the Societies of the People
Called Methodists.[9]

For all her many acts of service, the following meditation and prayer, written by Susanna, express so beautifully the richness of her fellowship with the Lord. Surely, her secret place with God was her most treasured place!

Meditations by Susanna Wesley

I give God the praise for any well-spent day. But I am yet unsatisfied, because I do not enjoy enough of God. I apprehend myself at too great a distance from him; I would have my soul more closely united to him by faith and love. I can appeal to his omniscience, that I would love him above all things. He that made me knows my desires, my expectations.

My joys all center in him, and it is he himself that I desire; it is his favor, it is his acceptance, the communications of his grace, that I earnestly wish for more than anything in the world; and I have no relish or delight in anything when under apprehensions of his displeasure.

I rejoice in my relationship to him, that he is my Father, my Lord, my God. I rejoice that he has power over me, and I desire to live in subjection to him; that he condescends to punish me when I transgress his laws, as a father chastens the son whom he loves. I thank him that he has brought me thus far; and I will beware of despairing of his mercy for the time which is yet to come, but will give God the glory of his free grace.[10]

Peace Like a River

Help me, O Lord, to make true use of all disappointments and calamities in this life, in such a way that they may unite my heart more closely with you.

Cause them to separate my affections from worldly things and inspire my soul with more vigor in the pursuit of true happiness.

Until this temper of mind be attained, I can never enjoy any settled peace, much less a calm serenity.

You only, O God, can satisfy my immortal soul and bestow those spiritual pleasures that alone are proper to its nature.

Grant me grace to stay and center my soul in you; to confine its desire, hopes, and expectations of happiness to you alone; calmly to attend to the seasons of your providence and to have a firm, habitual resignation to your will.

Enable me to love you, my God, with all my heart, with all my mind, with all my strength; so to love you as to desire you; so to desire you as to be uneasy without you, without your favor, without some such resemblance to you as my nature in this imperfect state can bear. Amen.[11]

Endnotes

1. Kathy McReynolds, *Susanna Wesley, Women Of Faith*, (Minneapolis MN: Bethany House Publishers, copyright 1998.), 68-70.

2. Ibid. 94.

3. Ibid. 94.

4. Ibid. 95.

5. Ibid. 95-96.

6. Bruce L. Shelley, *Church History in Plain Language* (Waco, TX: Word Books; 1982) 354.

7. Ibid. 106.

8. Ibid. 119.

9. Ibid. 120.

10. Ibid. 155-156.

11. Ibid. 157-158.

Bibliography

Women of Awakenings, The Historic Contribution of Women to Revival Movements, by Lewis and Betty Drummond, Kregel Publications, copyright 1997.

CHAPTER 7

BASILEA SCHLINK (1904–2001):
GOD SENT ME TO THE CROSS

~

While Basilea Schlink set out to discover the world as a young German woman, Hitler's influence was beginning to emerge within the fabric of German history. She began her studies in social welfare in 1923, at the same time Hitler was attempting his first revolution, severely shaking the economy and creating inflation and the rationing of bread. As her nation was shaken to the core by political upheaval, Basilea's heart experienced its own kind of unrest. She was coming to grips with interior issues of true humility and repentance from sin, pride, and ambition.

She stated, "In my childhood and early youth it was always the same. When my sinful nature sought satisfaction, God sent me a cross so that a part of me had to die."[1]

Born in Darmstadt, Germany on October 21, 1904, Basilea's heart from an early age was turned toward the Lord. Although she was high-spirited and enjoyed many activities as other girls of her age, the call of God echoed deep in her soul. At the age of 20, Basilea's prayer was, "Preserve this inner life, but take away my self-esteem. All that I have comes from You and all the good in me can only be attributed to You, Lord Jesus. That I know very well."[2]

As a young woman, Basilea longed for someone to lead her to God. Finding no one, she worked hard to improve herself. Living without the transforming power of God soon brought her to the end of her striving. She realized she needed a revelation of God in her heart. In August 1922, God answered her plea and she beheld Jesus inwardly as the crucified Lord. She knew that she had come into the saving knowledge of Jesus Christ!

Revelation of the Father's love began to flow into her. The mystery of the grace of God unfolded in her heart and undid the works of the flesh. From this experience was birthed deep desire. Basilea longed to learn how to pray and grow in God's love. During these early days, Jesus Himself led her and taught her. She became aware that the former activities that brought her pleasure actually grieved the Holy Spirit, and so out of love for Him she let go of those things.

Treasures of the Heart

Basilea's devotion grew as she matured into adulthood and God deposited many treasures into her heart. She learned that God would reveal Himself to her to the extent that she would allow His Word to convict her heart. God spoke to her of the need to come to the end of self and to walk in repentance so that the death that sin produces would be broken off, and new life result. By experiencing greater dimensions of His love, her heart became increasingly sensitive to those things precious to His wonderful heart. Oh, for more of His love within us!

The purifying process continued in Basilea as the Lord brought His light to the motives of her heart. Why did she want to help people? Was she giving them her love, or God's love? She was learning the absolute need to love people with divine love, because human love is impure and limited. Divine love is constant and sure; it does not waiver with the ebb and flow of human emotions and circumstances. Basilea learned that we must give Him the highest place, not because of any desire to minister to others, but because of love for Him alone! Our hearts and our lives must be centered on Him, solely because He is our delight!

Peeling an Onion

During her university years as she completed her studies and then turned to teaching, she experienced mountain peaks and valleys with the Lord. At times she felt very alone. It seemed that God was silently asking her, "Am I enough for you even when it feels like I'm dead, even when I do not give you inner consolation or loving proofs of My presence?"[3]

As Basilea allowed the Lord's piercing question go deep into her spirit, she was convicted of her sin and asked for His forgiveness. He transformed her heart to experience true thankfulness, and gratitude for His goodness and faithfulness spilled over from her soul.

Like unpeeling the skin of an onion, He was dealing with issues of her heart, layer by layer, exposing darkness she didn't even know was there. By His great love and wonderful compassion, He was bringing her to the light! Exposing darkness of the soul requires time in the valleys, in dark and lonely places. It's there that His glorious light shines the very brightest!

In 1930 Basilea attended the University in Berlin to work on her Ph.D. in psychology. She lived part of this time with Erika, her true spiritual friend. During this time, Basilea felt convicted to live a celibate life. She sensed that God planned for she and Erika to found and build up a ministry in His Kingdom.

In 1933, at the height of Nazi National Socialism, Basilea's Jewish professors were forced to relinquish their positions. From 1933 to 1935, this young student held the position of national president of the Women's Division of the German Student Christian Movement. As providence would have it, Basilea was used to influence the branch of the Christian student group, called the Confessing Church, to reject an Aryan paragraph stating that only German girls would be permitted to attend the meetings.

Courageous Faith

Hebrew Christian students would continue to be accepted within these circles, which meant that their entire organization could be dissolved. Basilea was beginning to step out in courageous faith to stand up for the Jewish people under the Nazis.

Trials, poverty, and hardships followed in the years from 1936 to 1938. Basilea and Erika moved to Darmstadt where they felt they were to begin a Bible training course for women who were to become pastors' wives or go into ministry themselves. With no way of earning a living, the two young women trusted God for every need. They lived in real poverty, and dug into God for their continual sustenance and spiritual development. By the end of the second year, a handful of women had completed their course.

By the fall of 1938, with no money and no women registering for their course, it seemed the dream had died. But at the last moment a couple of local pastors pulled together some financial aid to help fund youth work. Although Basilea started the girls' youth ministry, it quickly grew to 100 members under Erika's leadership. Basilea, now in her mid-30s, had no ministry, nothing.

Frontline Courage

Suddenly, in 1939, the Missionary Society for Moslems asked Basilea to take over its traveling lectureship. So, during these desperate, bloody years of war throughout Europe, Basilea traveled in crowded trains and endured blackouts, severe coal shortages, and bombing raids. In the frigid winter of 1940-41, she traveled for four weeks across Prussia, where the temperatures were -20 to -40 degrees Fahrenheit. Wherever she went, God was her faithful and constant companion, her security and her peace throughout this entire time.

Sometimes informers were present in her meetings, but she continued to feel compelled to speak of God's plan of salvation for the Jews, and of His special covenant with them. Twice she was reported by these informants and interrogated for hours by the secret police. Still, God kept her safe, and she was not arrested. Her Bible studies were allowed to continue even though both the Old and New Testaments were taught, which was forbidden under Hitler.

As Basilea traveled from place to place, she spoke on the power of Jesus' blood, His victory over the enemy, and His triumphant return. She covered Jesus' second coming, God's plan of salvation for Israel and the city of God, Heaven and hell, the blessings of suffering, and how to overcome.

For years, she prayed: "Grant me love, love which is not irritable or resentful, which bears all things, hopes all things, believes all things, endures all things."[4] God taught her the way of humility, to cease from self-justification, and to endure with patience and forbearance. His perfect love was to become her life's message!

Revival

On September 11, 1944, an air raid was leveled against Darmstadt. Buildings were toppled everywhere! Yet this black cloud contained a silver lining. It so sobered the girls with whom Erika and Basilea had been working that the change in their lives unleashed revival in their area.

These young women were seized with the intense need for personal repentance! As they spent more time in prayer, the Lord dealt with Erika and Basilea concerning the sins of their nation. During the war years, they had spent time in prayer over personal issues, but had they cried out for national sins? Had they repented for the prisoners of war, and for the millions of Jews who were slaughtered?

They had thought they were devoting their lives to God, but had they seen their lives in light of the sin of their nation? Great conviction fell upon them. Revival came from the ashes of Darmstadt!

Now the stage was being set for the foundation of a dream held within Basilea's heart. It would be called "The Sisterhood of Mary." It would grow to be a community of women living in an attitude of contrition and fellowship in bridal love for Jesus. They would stand in the gap for their nation. Identifying Germany's sins as their own, the Sisters of Mary would cry out for mercy and forgiveness.

The Sisterhood of Mary

On March 30, 1947, the dream became a reality. The Sisterhood was established, founded by Basilea and Paul Riedinger, a Methodist church leader. It would have Lutheran roots, but eventually become interdenominational. The early days saw valleys, dark places, criticism, questionings, lack, and even sickness.

Often, Basilea retreated into seclusion with God. She spent weeks rarely seeing or talking to anyone. During such times she experienced the sweet presence of God and the sense of eternity resting in her room. In times of seclusion, she received revelations from God concerning His nature, or the Scripture. Many times He would direct her into serious assignments that would take much prayer to be accomplished.

The Sufferings of Jesus

Basilea gained understanding into the sufferings of Jesus, and learned that loneliness is one of the ways He suffered while here on earth. The Lord would come to her in those times and share burdens of His heart with her.

He spoke to her of His pain that His Body was not one. This sent her on many missions to build up and repair the breach. Many times she went to various parts of the Body of

Christ, in an attitude of humility and repentance, asking for forgiveness. She was often met with divisive words, but sometimes true reconciliation took place. She was a true forerunner, who not only understood the power and importance of identificational repentance but actually did it!

In May 1949, Mother Basilea (as she was called), felt inspired to build a chapel for Jesus, where He would be adored. The Sisters of Mary also needed a house where new sisters could join the ministry. When they started these projects, they only had 30 marks! Nevertheless, the Lord was their banker. Both buildings were completed, and the chapel was built from bricks salvaged from the ruins of the city. This home God provided for the Sisterhood became known as Kanaan.

During one of her times of seclusion, she received a commission from God to speak to the Pope. She was to go and discuss God's desire for all His Body to become one. Specifically, she would discuss the breach between Protestants and Roman Catholics.

Before she could go, much work would need to be completed. She learned that the enemy's attacks always correspond to the spiritual significance of the commission. She learned to identify with the words of Paul: "I rejoice in my suffering for your sake, and in my flesh I complete what is lacking in Christ's afflictions."

Basilea learned to suffer for the unity of love. The inner conflicts she endured were an essential part of preparing for this assignment, because man's mind is full of corruption, opinion, and faultfinding. She submitted her own mind anew and fresh to the blood and the lordship of Jesus. Through prayer, she was able to attain a private audience with Pope

Pius XII. Her assignment was fulfilled. She could not determine his response, but she had faithfully answered God's call to be a voice echoing the ache in God's heart! The Pope responded to her, "Is that really the Savior's wish?"[5]

The seeds we are asked to sow take time to germinate. We don't know when the fruit will be evident. Hence, it requires of us, the sowers, to be patient and always to have an eternal perspective. God's seeds always grow! This is yet another Kingdom principal that God birthed deep in Basilea's spirit!

After her trip to Rome, the Lord opened up branches for The Sisterhood of Mary in England, Greece, and Italy. The work crossed denominational borders into the Anglican, Greek Orthodox, and Roman Catholic churches. Eventually, branches would include more than 200 women from 20 countries, with 14 men in the Canaan Franciscan Brothers.

God's Heart for Israel

In other times of seclusion beginning in 1954, God spoke to Basilea about His heart for Israel, His specially chosen people. A cry for God's people arose from her heart towards the throne of mercy, "Awaken souls amongst Your chosen people Israel to love You like a bride so that one day they may be with You in the City of God."[6]

With this call came the realization that Germany, Basilea's homeland, had committed horrible atrocities against the Jewish people. By doing so, they had heaped terrible guilt upon themselves! As she entered into specific times of prayer and fasting concerning this overpowering weight of sin, the light of God broke through. No longer did the sisters avoid houses they knew belonged to Jewish families because of guilt or shame. With God's renewed love in their hearts, they visited these families, asking for forgiveness on behalf of their nation. Repentance began to do the work of reconciliation.

When the sisters desired to visit Israel an invitation was required in order to issue visas because of their German citizenship. The door was opened; an invitation came to the doorstep. They obtained the necessary visas and walked through the land of Israel, asking God's forgiveness for Germany's sin. Their labors toward reconciliation resulted in sending two sisters there to live in 1957. Basilea went on to write a book calling Christians to an awareness of its sins against the Jews.

Later, an additional branch of the Sisters of Mary was established in Jerusalem, called Beth Abraham. These events brought invitations from Jewish communities within the United States and Canada for Basilea to speak in their synagogues. Rabbis and students attended her meetings.

The Valley of the Shadow of Death

In 1959, Basilea suffered from a serious heart condition. Inwardly, she felt she was being led through the valley of the shadow of death. After releasing her will into God's will for her life, she received an assurance from God that she would recover. The Lord granted health to her, and she became stronger than before. Soon after this trial, she wrote the book, *Repentance—The Joy Filled Life* (Bethany House, 1984). She understood that "a person lacking contrition lacks everything. If he has contrition and repentance, he has everything he needs, for repentance draws down God's grace."[7]

In 1959 came another call from God concerning the land of Israel. Basilea was to spend time in the Holy Land seeking out the places where Jesus lived and suffered in order to pray for an awakening of God's purposes for those places. As she traveled through the land, she felt the grief of Jesus Christ, because His people remained so unmoved towards the places He lived His earthly life. Little was being done to keep these sights holy.

Basilea spent time in prayer in Gethsemane at Lithostrotos, where Christ was crowned with thorns, and at the Kidron Valley, where He was led away as a prisoner. Here she experienced a living encounter with God and wrote many songs, devotional readings, and texts. She compiled these writings into books for pilgrims visiting these sites. Booklets and leaflets were created from her book and distributed by thousands at the holy sites, as well as given away at various hotels. Now the Sisters of Mary would begin hosting spiritual pilgrimages of the Holy Land.

A few years later, the Sisters were permitted to place plaques at the holy sites. Each one was inscribed with devotional thoughts to help visitors open their hearts to God in these places.

Memorials to God's Glory

After the enthusiastic success of the memorial plaques in Israel, Basilea and her sisters began praying about a new project in her own country of Germany. The Sisters of Mary sought permission to erect plaques at various scenic points to bring glory to God in the atmosphere of His most beautiful and stunning creation.

After the plaques were erected, stories were told of many individuals who were kept from committing suicide because of their presence. Eventually, this project became an international effort, with plaques being placed at points of majestic beauty in many nations!

Basilea accomplished many things during her lifetime, much more than can be accounted for here. Nevertheless, her primary goal was to love Jesus and to call others to love Him as our wonderful Bridegroom should be loved! All her many works were birthed out of this place of devotion in her heart for Him. The effects of her love and devotion will continue to bless many nations in the years to come.

Basilea went to be with the Lord on March 21, 2001, but her work and vision for the Sisterhood of Mary continues. This community is dedicated to Christian radio ministry and to Christian literature. The Sisterhood publishes tracts in 90 languages, which are distributed on five continents. Radio and television programs are broadcast in 23 languages. But more important than the programs and all the efforts is the fire of His love and the call to the secret place.

That privileged cry continues to echo across generations and ages of time! Let's turn now to hear its message to our own generation through the lives of those who have cultivated blessed friendship in the secret place.

Endnotes

1. Basilea Schlink, *I Found The Key To The Heart Of God, My Personal Story*, (Minneapolis, MN: Bethany House Publishers, 1975), 19.

2. Ibid. 33.

3. Ibid. 74.

4. Ibid. 108.

5. Ibid. 212.

6. Ibid. 217.

7. Ibid. 265.

Bibliography

Behold His Love, by Basilea Schlink, Dimension Books published by Bethany Fellowship, Inc. Minneapolis, Minnesota, copyright 1973.

Father Of Comfort, by Basilea Schlink, Bethany Fellowship, Inc. Minneapolis, Minnesota, copyright 1971.

I Found The Key To The Heart Of God, My Personal Story, by Basilea Schlink, Bethany House Publishers, Minneapolis, Minnesota, copyright 1975.

In Whom The Father Delights, Growing Closer to God through Suffering, by Basilea Schlink, Chosen Books, Old Tappen, New Jersey, copyright 1987.

Websites include:

http://www.kanaan.org/Mother.htm "Who is M. Basilea Schlink? Who is M. Martyria Madauss?

http://www.kanaan,org/main_contents.htm "Welcome to the home page of Evangelical Sisterhood of Mary!

http://www.gospelcom.net/apologeticsindex/news1/an010403-21.html "Obituary: Mother Basilea Schlink-News about religious cults and sects"

SECTION THREE

FRIENDS OF THE SECRET PLACE

CHAPTER 8

GWEN SHAW:
A PASSION FOR NATIONS

~

"The burden of the Lord is the most overwhelming, life-changing thing that you can experience; and it can be a lifelong experience. When the burden of the Lord lifts, it is time to GO HOME!"[1]

The fiery passion to make God's heart and presence known among the nations continues to burn brightly in this dear woman of God whom I'm about to present to you. The stateswoman who made this statement is nearly 80 years old and is still a globetrotter for Jesus. I'd like to begin this final section, *Friends of the Secret Place*, by introducing you to this wonderful lady I consider my friend, who has been first and foremost a friend of the beloved Bridegroom and of His secret place for many years.

Gwen Shaw has ministered in more than 100 nations and is founder of the End-Time Handmaidens, an organization that has lit the pathway to the secret place for nearly a generation.

Born to Serve the Lord

Loving and serving her Lord was her destiny. Gwendolyn Ruth had parents who dedicated her to the Lord from the womb. She was born to serve the Lord.

Gwen's mother came from a godly family of sincere Mennonites who had served the Lord for many generations. These God-fearing forefathers paid a terrible price for their testimony. Years earlier, these new believers were banished from their beautiful homes in the Emmental Valley of the Swiss Alps because of their conviction that salvation was by grace.

The teachings of Martin Luther had swept across Europe and changed their lives forever. Many of the faithful died as martyrs, being burned at the stake or speared through. Young men were sold as galley slaves, and old fathers were left to die in dark dungeons. Gwen's ancestors were forced to leave their homes and live a life of wandering for decades until Russia opened its doors. There they found what they desired more than anything else: religious freedom.[2]

During the first bitter Russian winter in their new homeland, they existed by digging holes in the ground and living under the earth. Gradually, they began to raise crops and prosper until they finally owned their own homes. Towns and villages of German-speaking people, all of them seeking religious freedom, arrived in Russia.[3]

When all seemed to be going well the Lord visited His people and warned them through the gift of prophecy that great persecution was coming to Russia. This persecution would be greater than any they had ever known in the past, and for those who stayed there would be no survivors. God told them to leave Russia and go to a new homeland. Some heeded the word of the Lord, while others mocked it and were left behind. Sadly, these endured unspeakable suffering and death.

This is how Gwen came to be born in Canada. Her grandfather, Peter Miller (Mueller), (her mother's father) and others traveled to Canada as a young man in obedience to the word of the Lord. These hardworking farmers grew wheat from the grain that they brought with them from the bread-basket of Russia.[4] So Gwen grew up attending the Emmanuel Mennonite Church in Saskatchewan, founded by her grand-father in the middle prairie province of Canada. Here her parents fell in love, married, and dedicated their three chil-dren to the Lord—Gwen, Earl, and Jamie. The entire family faithfully attended the church built on the land dedicated by Grandfather Miller.

In her middle teens, Gwen grew bored with rural prairie life and escaped with a friend to the big city. While she was away, her family was dramatically impacted by the Pente-costal movement, sweeping through the community. Gwen was attending a more liberal congregation where sin was sel-dom mentioned and people felt free to live any way they wanted.

After a few months of rebellion and desperate prayers by her family, Gwen came back to the Lord and was glorious-ly filled with the Holy Spirit. She then went off to the Assem-bly of God (Pentecostal Assemblies of Canada) Bible School in Ontario to be trained for the Lord's work.

At school, revival fire fell among the students, and in the midst of this outpouring God called Gwen to China. Visions, spiritual gifts, intercession, and deep conviction of the Lord's presence flowed freely during those special days. But somewhat ignorantly, Gwen had married a young man who was not as fervent about God's purposes. Gwen prayed and prayed. Eventually, the Lord moved on his heart, and so in obedience they went off as faith missionaries to a distant land.

Launching Out Into the Deep

Gwen launched out to the mission field of China as a very young woman. It was December 16, 1947 when she landed in Shanghai just having turned 23 years old. In obedience, she answered the call of God upon her life and received a passionate burden from the Lord for the Chinese people.

Sometimes that burden was greater than at other times. As the years went by and China fell into the hands of Communism, the doors for the gospel in Mainland China slammed shut. Even so, Gwen continued to serve the Lord among the Chinese people in Taiwan and Hong Kong, not missing a step in fulfilling that call of God. Never for a moment did she think of turning back from that call.

This dear pioneer loved the Chinese, and she considered them her people. She has often stated, "I belonged to them, and their need was my need; their pain, my pain."[5] In fact, Gwen had been God's spokeswoman, used to warn and foretell the closing of the nation of China to missionary work long before it ever fell to the communists.[6] The fact that Gwen heard this prophetic utterance doubtless fueled the flame of passion within her heart. This Canadian volunteer reached out to China with a deep sense of urgency.

As life unfolded, ten years of marriage had come and gone and then came the arrival of three precious sons: David, Danny, and Tommy. And as with many mothers of young children, Sister Gwen's life was now occupied with family affairs. Gwen admits that it was hard to be a mother of three frisky, lively boys and still keep her missionary vision alive. But with the help of an "ahman," (housemaid and nanny) the boy's early years were spent growing up in the mission field of Hong Kong.

One day in 1963, after 16 years of missionary service God met her with a new and wonderful anointing. She witnessed the power of God in the lives of ordinary people who paid a price, fasted, and prayed for a fresh anointing. Fresh desire arose in her heart. Gwen hungered for more of God, and she longed for her life to make a difference. So, she dedicated her life afresh to God. From that point on it would be 100 percent, complete, unconditional, and total surrender to His will—whatever the cost! Guess what happened? As with many others, God took her up on the vow she made to Him.

A Fresh Anointing Renewed My Vision

After 16 years of faith, trials, and blessings, God renewed His great calling in Gwen's life. This time it was not only to go to China, but to all the nations of the world. Never in her wildest dreams did she ever imagine all that God had planned for her. "I simply put my hand in His and began to follow Him step-by-step, day-by-day, and nation by nation."[7] Gwen bravely preached the gospel, but did so at great cost—a cost that would fix her eyes on Jesus, the Lover of her soul.

With this new and wonderful anointing came a tremendous burden for souls and an overwhelming vision for the nations.

That fresh call took her to various parts of China, Mongolia, Taiwan, the Philippines, and on to Indonesia where she saw the Lord do great miracles of deliverance and salvation. She would minister among the Presbyterians in one location, the Pentecostal Assemblies in another, with Catholic nuns and Orthodox priests, as well as the Methodists, Baptists, Missionary Alliance, Salvation Army, and whoever was hungry for more of God. Wherever the Spirit said, "Come," Sister Gwen went.

During the children's summer vacation, Gwen often would take one of them with her when she went to minister. Nine-year-old David, the oldest, who played the trumpet always knew how to get a crowd. He would borrow someone's bicycle, ride out to the marketplace and play his trumpet while passing out tracts and flyers about the meetings. Turning towards the gathering, he would encourage them to come and hear his mother preach. And preach she did! They had great times together.

The Terrible Price

On other occasions the children had to attend school and Gwen was forced to go it alone. Long before the fresh double-portion anointing had come upon Gwen, her relationship with her husband had grown apart in vision and calling, resulting in a painful separation of ways. The Lord used this pain redemptively, as a part of a breaking process that took Gwen into a deeper place with God where He alone became her husband, shelter, and refuge.

At times Gwen's loneliness became so acute that it pierced into her heart like a knife. None but God knew the tears, pain, loneliness, and longing—the price she paid to fulfill her vow to God!

At one point, she started to make excuses to try to escape God's call, and she nearly lost all three of her boys. Danny almost drowned in the South China Sea. David slipped right in front of a fast, oncoming car; and Tommy was miraculously rescued out of a river that was more like a stagnant pond filled with sewage. Nevertheless, the Lord promised His protection and to be their Father if she would but follow Him.

Gwen knew that God was speaking loud and clear, warning her of how costly it could be to put anything before Him—even her children. The price might be more costly than the one she was already paying. So again, she counted the cost and said yes to her Lord. That's when she turned her gaze towards His and received her next assignment—India.

India, My Great Love

India became Gwen's great love. She often would say, "China was my first love, and India was my great love."[8] No words could describe what it meant to feel God's heartbeat of love for a nation. She would have gladly laid down her whole life for the Lord in India. In fact, that became her desire.

In this season of her life, she experienced one of the greatest joys of service to God. Those who know their God take action. So, Gwen raised a tent in many parts of northern India and openly preached the gospel of the Lord Jesus Christ as a woman on the frontlines. What joy to see people respond to the mercy of God! How exciting to lead many Hindu and Muslims to the Lord Jesus Christ!

Here on India's frontline, Gwen translated her tract *Who Is Jesus?* into the Bengali language[9] as she ministered from Punjab to Calcutta, New Delhi to Allahabad, and from coast to coast. Her father and brother joined in those mighty harvest fields of souls under the big tent. Gwen played an accordion and brother Earl joined her in singing songs of Zion. The cost was great, but revival was in the air.

Gwen's travels didn't stop in India. Next came Russia, and once again God's heart of passion for the lost beat inside her as if it were her own. Miraculously, she was the first woman to preach in the Baptist Church in Moscow. Like the apostolic ambassadors of old, Gwen would pray, fast, and agonize for the nations. When no door was open to her, God would be the door. When no finances existed, He would be her provider.

Jesus became the doorkeeper of the nations, opening entry to Finland, Bali, Denmark, Norway, Sweden, England, Germany, Africa, Pakistan, the United States, and Canada. If you could pronounce it, Jesus, her husbandman took this little Canadian lady there. He introduced her to kings and paupers, princesses and lepers, and she shared freely to all, the timeless story of God's great grace and wonderful love.

Argentina, the Womb of the End-Time Handmaidens

You ask the question, "How much can one heart contain?" Remember, "For God so loved the world..." If God's love is in your heart, then your heart will expand to be like His. This is just what happened in Sister Gwen.

Her next call came and she went to Argentina where once again she felt the heartbeat of God, now for the Spanish-speaking people of that great land. Throughout Argentina, she saw the mighty hand of God working with mighty displays of supernatural power following the preaching of His Word.

Then one night in Buenos Aires, something happened that was destined to change many lives. Gwen had just ministered in a large Assembly of God church where God had poured out His Spirit. Miracles of healing had taken place, and people had seen angels. God's tangible, manifested presence had come down to be among them. No one wanted to leave the meetings as the God of the secret place was now being revealed openly.

When Gwen went back tired and exhausted to the lonely hotel room that night, she lay there on her bed. Looking up to God, she asked Him a question. "God, how can You use me? I am nothing. I make mistakes. I am far from perfect. Yet I have seen Your glory like a trail of fire following me everywhere. How? Why?"

An amazing thing happened; He answered! "It's because you are willing to do anything I ask you to do!" With the curiosity of a child, Gwen inquired, "Is that all, Lord? Then You could use anyone, any woman, who like myself would be totally surrendered to You!"

"Yes, My child, I could," He answered.

Strengthened in faith, Gwen responded, "Then, Lord, raise up ten thousand women—women just like myself who will pay any price, make any sacrifice, and be totally obedient to Your will."[10] The year was 1966 when this cry of birthing was heard in the night.

The End of the Road

Four years later, after she had ministered in many other nations all over the world, Gwen found herself in Chicago at the end of the road. Her children were in Hong Kong. Her marriage was over. Her heart was broken, and she was sure that she could never serve God again. Her emotions were crashing, as the enemy whispered that no one would accept a woman whose marriage had fallen apart!

"I did the only thing I knew to do. I went back to the drawing board, back to the Cross."[11] Gwen underwent another 21-day fast and waited upon the Lord. He spoke once more. Night after night the Lord, her husbandman, came to her releasing His plans, visiting her by His angels, answering all her questions.

To confirm these encounters, the Lord of Hosts sent a prophet to tell her that she must begin to call out the End-Time Handmaidens. God said there was an army of women out there in the background, standing "idle in the market-place, whom no one had hired." They were waiting to hear the call to go out and serve the Lord in the harvest fields of the world.

Perhaps no one knew those harvest fields better than Sister Gwen. Already, she had been to many of the nations of the world. Often it's when we think "it's all over" that God reveals that He is everything, and we are but His servants. It happened that way with Gwen; perhaps it has happened that way with you, too.

The Beginning of a New Calling

With fresh resolve, faith, and obedience Gwen began to give the call to women everywhere to join her in sharing her burden for souls. A living organism was born—one full of consecration, holiness, and the Word of the Lord. The End-Time Handmaidens rose up from nation to nation as the Holy Spirit prepared women's hearts around the world in the same way He had prepared hers. God's daughters would fast and pray; in brokenness they would wait and wonder if God really even knew their names. Then, from the stillness in the depth of God's wonderful presence He called their names. End-Time Handmaidens were commissioned into the harvest, with hearts burning brightly, radiating the glow of holiness from the secret place.

But the Lord did not forget his handmaiden Gwen. He sent to her a "Simon" to help her carry the cross and lighten the load. At a time of fellowship in Santa Barbara, California, Gwen met Lieutenant Colonel James von Doornum Shaw, a retired Baptist USAF pilot and officer.

When she saw him, the Holy Spirit told her to go and lay hands upon this stranger and prophesy to him. Reluctantly, she obeyed and declared to this Baptist man that God was bringing him into a new consecration. Times of satisfaction and joy from the Holy Spirit were waiting for him like none he had never known. She declared that as he had flown in the natural, so would he fly in the spiritual realm. Gwen spoke the word "completeness" over this man.

Jim Shaw went on a fast to seek the face of the Lord, and a new heart for missions bubbled up in him. Little did Gwen realize that she would end up marrying this wonderful man who had flown numerous aircraft for well over 30 years! Together they would fly to many nations serving the Lord together. The End-Time Handmaidens would also become complete by adding the End-Time Servants as well. And so they both became "completed" and have served the Master together for close to 30 glorious years now.

Looking Back

Many years have passed since Gwen first gave her heart to the Lord. She was but 17 years old then. For more than 60 years she has known, loved, and served her Master. Listen to her heart as she shares her burden with you.

"If I could live my life over again, I would give it all to God again. God has given me supernatural strength to fulfill a supernatural calling. But, as hard as I work and as fast as I run, I can't keep up with Him. I have now been to over one hundred nations and still they keep calling."

"Day after day they're calling, calling, calling. This call to the nations is there, ringing in my ears, burning in my heart. I want to go, but I'm getting older now. I can't preach four and five times a day as I used to in Indonesia. I can understand the heart's cry of Moses when he said, 'I am not able to bear all this people alone, because it is too heavy for me' (Num. 11:14 KJV).

"Yes, it is getting too heavy for me. This terrible burden for Cambodia, North Korea, Tibet, Zambia, Pakistan, Albania, Chile, Iceland, and all the nations where I have not yet told the old, old story of Jesus and His love—besides the nations where I want to return again! Moses wept. I weep too!

"Then I hear God say to me what He said to Moses, 'I will take of the spirit which is upon thee, and will put it upon them; and they shall bear the burden of the people with thee, that thou bear it not thyself alone' " (Num. 11:17b KJV).[12]

Will You Share Her Burden?

Sovereignly and supernaturally, God wants to put upon your life this same burden that He placed on Gwen Shaw's. Are you willing to accept it? Are you willing to share God's burden for the lost souls of the world?

It will not be easy. It will cost you everything. The tribe of Levi had no earthly inheritance. The Lord was their inheritance. You need to make the same dedication. You need to surrender totally to the will of God. Only then can He use you anywhere, anytime, in any way.

Today, right now, you may be wondering why you are alive. You feel you have no real reason for living, and that anyone could do your work as well as you do—or even better.

I beg you, please don't waste your life. Answer that call of God that has been there since you were in your mother's womb. Step up to the plate. Be a person who builds a private history before the throne of God and then watches with eager anticipation to see what the Master will do.

God's Word says to you, "Before I formed thee in the belly I knew thee; and before thou camest forth out of the womb I sanctified thee, and I ordained thee a prophet unto the nations" (Jer. 1:5 KJV).

You say, "I can't do it."

God says, "Say not, I am a child: for thou shalt go to all that I shall send thee, and whatsoever I command thee thou shalt speak" (Jer. 1:7 KJV).

You say, "I'm not talented. I have no gift to preach."

God says, "Behold, I have put My words in thy mouth."

Total Surrender.

Will you join Gwen and other women of the secret place in unconditional surrender to the glorious Father of the Lord Jesus Christ? If so, then pray the following statement composed by our modern-day pioneer who carries His presence to the nations.

> Lord, I give myself to You;
> I give my life to You.
> I feel Your call;
> I believe I was sent
> To do the will of my Father.
> I will take orders from You.
> I will submit to You.
> I will let You break my will.
> I will not seek for comfort
> Nor high position,
> Nor to do what I want to do.
> I love You, Jesus;
> I thank You for calling me,
> And that You want me,
> And that You can use me;
> And all I can say is,
> "Send the fire and burn up the sacrifice.
> Fill me with Thy Holy Spirit
> And give me a double portion of Thine anointing."[13]

Do you want to join in with the throngs of other pioneers who have gone before us? Do you want to be a dwelling place for God? Then follow the footsteps of Madame Jeanne Guyon and Teresa of Avila; draw near like Susanna Wesley and Fannie Crosby. Etch your name beside the likes of Basilea Schlink and Sister Gwen Shaw. You are a great candidate to be a friend of the secret place of the Most High.

Endnotes

1. Gwen R. Shaw, *Share My Burden* (Jasper, Arkansas: Engetal Press, 1984), 2.

2. Ibid, 3.

3. Ibid.

4. Gwen R. Shaw, *Unconditional Surrender: My Life Story*, (Jasper, Arkansas: Engetal Press, 1986), 5.

5. Gwen R. Shaw, *Share My Burden* (Jasper, Arkansas: Engetal Press, 1984), 2.

6. Gwen R. Shaw, *Unconditional Surrender: My Life Story* (Jasper, Arkansas: Engetal Press, 1986), 65-66.

7. Gwen R. Shaw, *Share My Burden* (Jasper Arkansas: Engeltal Press, 1984), 4.

8. Ibid, 5.

9. Gwen R. Shaw, *Unconditional Surrender: My Life Story* (Jasper, Arkansas: Engetal Press, 1986), 128-129.

10. Ibid, 126.

11. Gwen R. Shaw, *Share My Burden* (Jasper Arkansas: Engeltal Press, 1984), 6.

12. Ibid, 7-8.

13. Gwen R. Shaw, *Unconditional Surrender: My Life Story* (Jasper, Arkansas: Engetal Press, 1986), 293-294.

Additional Reading Material

Gwen Shaw, *Daily Preparations For Perfection*, (Jasper, AR.: Engeltal Press, 1983).

Gwen Shaw, *Love: The Law of the Angels*, (Jasper, AR.: Engeltal Press, 1979).

CHAPTER 9

ELIZABETH ALVES:
THE GRANDMA OF THE PRAYER SHIELD

"I never wanted a ministry. All I ever wanted was to know Christ!" These words epitomize the heart and motive of our dear friend, and another intimate friend of the secret place, Beth Alves.

When you're sitting in a meeting listening to Beth speak, you might easily feel as if you're being ushered into her living room. Her mothering grace is calm and unassuming. Here is a woman who has traveled to over 30 nations speaking with rich and poor, to rulers and peasants, always faithfully bringing the life of Christ to countless thousands. Nevertheless, Beth Alves exudes the simplicity of those who love God. She knows that all her accomplishments are not really hers, but belong to Him, her beautiful Jesus!

Beth and her husband, Floyd, began the early years of their marriage with roots in the Lutheran church. In Beth's words, they were Lutherans first and Christians second. But God wasn't going to let it stay that way. He was about to invade their home.

Power From on High

Beth remembers a pivotal time within her family that was key to their spiritual awakening. Her daughter had been diagnosed with an inoperable brain tumor. As Beth watched her daughter become increasingly debilitated, she prayed night and day. Walking the floors, she pleaded, "Jesus, if You're the same yesterday, today, and forever; and if I called You and You would walk this floor, then You would heal my daughter." Finally, Beth's daughter got to the point at which she no longer could talk or swallow. She no longer recognized her father—her favorite person. The only person she did know was Beth.

One day Beth came into her daughter's room in the hospital and busied herself because she was so depressed. As she started to clean the bedside table drawer, she pulled out a Gideon Bible and opened it, longing for something special to read. Growing up in the church, she had learned many wonderful Bible stories, but she didn't really know the Bible. At the time, she thought that was what the preacher was paid for—to study the Bible and preach from it.

Beth loved the Lord, but just didn't know much about Him. Opening up the Bible, she uttered a prayer of desperation asking for something special from Him. As she turned the pages, she found a Scripture that said, "He that believes and is baptized shall be saved, and he that believes not will be damned. And these signs shall follow those who believe, in My name they'll cast out demons..."

Oh, Beth thought, *it's not Halloween. I certainly don't need that!* "In My name they'll speak with a new tongue." She looked at her daughter and thought, *I can't go to another country and learn a new tongue right now. I've got to take care of her here and now.* "They said they'd pick up serpents." *Now, God...You know that I'm afraid of snakes. I'd never do that!*

"If they eat or drink any deadly thing, they will recover." Finally, Beth's eyes fell on a part of the passage that would change her life forever. Slowly, absorbing every word, she read...

"You can lay hands on the sick and they will recover."

Aha! That's exactly what she needed! Beth laid the open Bible across her daughter's feet, as if she were showing God what He had written.

Carefully, tentatively placing her hands on the dying child's feet, Beth looked up to Heaven and declared aloud: "God...I'm doing it. It doesn't say pray. Here it says to lay hands on them."

Feeling a little more hopeful, she closed the Bible and finished cleaning out the drawer. The next morning, her daughter went in for another pneumo-encephalogram test. Beth had no guarantee her daughter would come out alive!

The doctors came out of the test with tears running down their faces. Panic filled her heart; Beth was afraid she had lost her daughter. They brought Beth's daughter to her room still under the anesthetic. Setting next to her emaciated daughter, Beth's hot tears rolled freely down her face and splashed onto her lap, soaking her dress.

As if dreaming, suddenly she heard, "Hey Mom, where's daddy? I'm hungry—let's eat." Beth's daughter was sitting up in bed—completely healed!

"What Would You Have Me to Do?"

This amazing experience sent Beth on a search for more of God. She cried out to Him continually for His help, desperately wanting to know Him as the One who is the same yesterday, today, and forever.

Then on Good Friday, 1970, another prayer was dramatically answered. The Lord appeared before her. She was putting on her pantyhose getting ready to go somewhere, when she looked up and saw the form of Jesus. Beth cried out, "My Lord Jesus Christ, what would You have me to do?"

A blanket of divine peace filled the room, and she heard the words, "Stand up, for thou art worthy through My Son, Jesus."

She had been lying on the floor looking up towards Him. His eyes were pools of liquid living love. Much more happened on that wonderful day, and all the events of that powerful visitation changed her life forever.

Learning to Walk the Walk

The Lord sent her to a man whom she had never heard of before, a Lutheran minister. He lived five hours away, and it took her two weeks to find him. This pastor explained what had happened to her. Beth had been speaking in tongues since she met the resurrected Savior but didn't know what it was. After the experience, she couldn't speak at all for three days, but neither did she want to talk. Tears of joy and wonder just flowed down her cheeks.

When she was finally able to explain to her husband what had happened, he became very concerned. He, together with their local Lutheran pastor, agreed that it was good for Beth to be seeing this other Lutheran pastor. After all, he was Lutheran, so he must be all right.

Beth and her husband went to see the Lutheran pastor and also a psychologist. Beth's husband, the local Lutheran pastor, and the psychologist decided that Beth had experienced a pseudo-religious experience before having a mental breakdown.

Meanwhile, Beth spent five days with her newly found pastor friend and his wife. They poured over Scripture around the clock, and she wrote down as much as possible. She had an insatiable hunger for the things of God.

As she was leaving, the new pastor friend told her, "Beth, you must go home, and you must pray often in the Spirit. They think you're crazy. I've had five calls from them, but you must pray to build yourself up in the Holy Spirit. That will be your keeping power. But whatever you do, don't do it in front of them or anybody else, because they won't understand. There is something that you must always remember Beth; go home and walk the walk before you talk the talk. People will follow after your walk, but you'll lose them with your talk."

When Beth got home she dicovered that her husband had taken her name off the charge accounts and the bank account. In those days, if the husband didn't want to be held responsible for his wife's debts, he had to write a letter and have it publicly published, which he did. In addition, her husband started working nights so he could watch her all day long. Beth, on the other hand, was like a champagne bottle that somebody had shaken and put the cap back on. She was bubbling over with joy, but now she dared not express it. Beth determined she would follow the wise advice of her new friend and walk the walk.

Secret Joy

The psychologist explained to her husband that with a pseudo-religious experience, people begin to feel dirty and are driven to get clean all the time. So, everyone watched Beth for this cue. Meanwhile, in an effort to not pray in front of anyone, Beth began to retreat to the bathroom and take four to six showers a day, so that she could pray in tongues in the shower. She was so full of joy that she was about to explode! However, this new behavior sent all the wrong messages to her husband.

The local Lutheran church relieved Beth of all her responsibilities, now viewing her as a threat. She lost her church friends, and her husband's friends became just his friends. She felt totally and completely alone. Communication between the couple disintegrated. He was running away from God as hard as she was running towards Him! Beth's husband and his mother even attempted to have the children taken away from her. They made plans to have her committed to an institution and give her shock treatments, thinking this was the only way to erase her religious fantasy from her mind.

In the Lion's Den

In the midst of this turmoil, the Lord led Beth to a woman who became her mentor. What should she do? Beth asked, fearing for her future in the face of the threat of being committed to an institution. Her mentor said, "Just remember this, Beth: Daniel trusted God in the lion's den, and God shut the lion's mouths. If you have to go to a mental institution, I'll pray that God shuts his mouth."

Her husband put her in the car, drove about six blocks, and came back home. "I can't do it," he said.

Beth and her husband lived the next two and a half years in great difficulty. Eventually, her husband received the baptism of the Holy Spirit by reading his Bible. After he had heard Beth talk and heard her pray he had gone to the Bible to check it out…and read himself right into Jesus!

Pathway to the Secret Place

On the day that God visited Beth, He baptized her with love for her husband. No matter how difficult her husband made life for her, she just loved him that much more. She would get hurt, but not angry. Beth had no one to talk to but her spiritual mom.

Beth's experience with God brought a seed of pride into her life. At least she thought so. She knew everything, but in reality she knew nothing. Completely alone, except for her children and her spiritual mentor, God was using these difficult times to burn out the dross in her heart. These were her beginnings with God, glorious and yet so difficult. The pathway to abiding in the secret place was a rocky, bumpy, painful road.

Rabbi—Teacher

"Lord, please help me; I don't have time to pray." The Lord was Beth's teacher in such practical ways. She had four daughters, adopted another, and cared for three more whose mother had died, and two other girls whose mother was in a mental hospital. Plus, Beth was working full time! She asked God, "When am I going to pray for those You've given me charge over?"

The Lord told her to make a list of everything she did every day. She listed washing dishes every morning, ironing, hanging out the clothes to dry on the clothesline, and making the bed. She took the list of household chores and assigned a name from her prayer list to each chore. When she would work on a particular chore she would pray for the person listed beside that chore.

At that time her husband wasn't walking with the Lord, so Beth admits that she assigned his name beside the chore of cleaning the commode. But then the Lord dealt with her attitude, and told her: "Beth, you came to the right place, because all those prayers belong in the pity pot." So, she shunned self-pity and began to bless her husband, her enemies, and those who hurt her. Eventually the commode became her bless-me pot.

A Gift of Intercession

Once when Beth was about to hang the clothes on the line a neighbor dropped by. While they drank some iced tea and talked, she kept thinking about how she needed to go and hang out those clothes. *But how rude that would seem*, she thought.

Suddenly, she jumped up and the basket of clothes went flying across the floor. "You have to excuse me. I've got a project to do. Just wait here. I'll be back."

Beth went to hang out the clothes, and as she did she started to weep, and then wail. She became so troubled that she had to cling to the clothesline pole to hold herself up. The person she had assigned to this chore was her daughter who was in junior high school. She prayed in the Spirit for this daughter, not knowing specifically what was happening. She glanced at the clock as she came back into the house.

Beth's daughter came home from school later that afternoon. As they were washing dishes together after dinner, Beth asked her daughter what happened to her at 2:15 p.m. Looking startled, her daughter began to cry and said that some kids had talked her into running away from school with them. At 2:15 she had gone to her locker to put her things away and get what she needed to leave with them. However, she found that she couldn't move. All she could do was stand there and cry. She closed her locker and went back to her class.

Beth was left with the joyful knowledge that God had used her that day to make a difference in her daughter's life. Had she not obeyed the inner prompting that comes from spending time with Him, she might have missed her God-given assignment!

Grandma of the Prayer Shield

"Lord, teach me to pray," became Beth's desperate cry in those early days. God faithfully answered her prayer. Over the years, the Lord has unfolded to Beth simple yet profound truths about prayer and intercession that she continues to impart to others. Thousands from many nations have been released into ministry as they have learned principles of prayer and prophecy. With gentleness, humor, and simplicity, she captures the hearts of her listeners, encouraging them that they, too, can hear the voice of the Lord.

In 1971, Beth sensed the Lord impressing upon her the importance of praying for spiritual leaders worldwide. Her vision was based on Isaiah 62:6–7, which says, "On your walls, O Jerusalem, I have appointed watchmen; all day and all night they will never keep silent. You who remind the

Lord, take no rest for yourselves; and give Him no rest until He establishes and makes Jerusalem a praise in the earth" (NAS).

Beth and her husband, Floyd, founded Intercessors International in 1972. Here, Beth has used her rich insights about prayer as a wonderful tool to shield leaders under a cover of loving, spiritual intercession. The Lord has taught Beth to pray, giving her much wisdom and extremely practical applications.

She has been called the "Grandma of the Prayer Shield." She has received great understanding about the need for our leaders to be covered in prayer. These leaders include ministers, missionaries, and business and spiritual leaders around the world. She teaches on many different types of intercessors, and with her great insight, is able to extend grace to others to flow in their own individually tailored intercessory gifts.

Godly Mentoring

Beth highly values the importance of godly mentoring. While her children were still young and at home, she turned down a significant opportunity from the Lord to start a prayer ministry. She felt it necessary to mentor her children and passed that opportunity onto another, believing that if the call truly was from God, it would still be there when her children were grown. It was.

According to Beth, oftentimes you lay the groundwork and others get the credit. That's a sign of a good mentor. You don't mentor to be somebody; you mentor because God gives you that privilege and that opportunity. A mentor is somebody God trusts. The word *mentor* means "teacher, guide, coach, trainer, and instructor." Nowhere does it say possessor. Mentors must never, ever dominate or control.

Being a mentor is like taking care of a baby whose bottle keeps falling out of his or her mouth. The baby burps all over you and makes a mess of things. But if you're the caretaker of that person, you'll make certain that the baby is fed.

You can't teach someone how to mentor in a class because mentoring is a heart-to-heart connection. Such connections are necessary to bring out the best in a person, identify his or her giftings, understand weaknesses, and help that individual turn those weaknesses into strengths. "Love bears all things," says Corinthians. And *bear* means "to carry or sustain." Love also believes all things, which indicates total faith and trust.

When the days of being mentored are over, there is a test before each of us. It's amazing how quickly pride pops up then. Graduation has come, right? That means the time for release!

A Servant's Heart

Sometimes we forget the simplest of things. We forget that Jesus spent His life here on earth teaching us how to serve. He was the greatest servant who ever lived.

We look for an explosion of power, signs, and wonders, and what does God do? In Beth's case, He sent her to be a servant and to keep the house of an evangelist. She had always employed people to clean her house, and then God sent her to clean someone else's. As she cleaned those commodes, she would cry and complain to God: "God, I've got a call on my life, and here I am scrubbing and dusting. How can I do my calling by cleaning these pots all day?"

The Lord answered her saying, "You came to the right place. You came to the pity pot." Conviction hit her heart, and she repented.

One day, the evangelist's wife asked Beth to pray with her, and God spoke through her in a profound way as they prayed together. Later the evangelist was called away to teach on prayer but couldn't go. So, he sent Beth in his place, and that's how she started in the work of the ministry.

Today, Beth pours out her life to help teach and mentor others. She has traveled extensively, teaching and ministering in seminars and conferences worldwide. She has participated in the March for Jesus in Berlin, Germany; her ministry was involved in "The Concert for the Lord in the heart of the Gobi Desert," and in Romania as they prayed about the injustices committed against the children. She has great proficiency and accuracy in delivering prophetic ministry, which has given her great credibility among world leaders. Beth is also well-known in Germany as she and Floyd lived there as missionaries.

Beth has authored *Becoming a Prayer Warrior, The Mighty Warrior: A Guide to Effective Prayer, Daily Prayers*, and booklets in the *Praying With Purpose* series. She has also co-authored *Intercessors: Discover Your Prayer Power.*

Beth is a core faculty member of Wagner Leadership Institute and Harvest Evangelism's City Reacher's School. She has served on the Spiritual Warfare Network and the board of directors of Aglow International. She has also been a part-time faculty member at Christ for the Nations Institute, Dallas, Texas.

Beth and her husband, Floyd, have four daughters and fifteen grandchildren. They live in Texas and are life-giving members in their local church.

Beth would not want this chapter to end focusing on her merits. Therefore, it would be appropriate to end with one of her prayers, the cry of her heart.

Father, let Your will be done, Your Kingdom come. There is so much information, Father. But we don't want information; we want that which will bring life to Your people, in the name of Jesus, and we give You the praise, honor, and glory in Jesus' name, Amen.

Bibliography

~

Intercessors; Discover Your Prayer Power, by Elizabeth Alves, Tommi Femrite, Karen Kaufman, copyright 2000. Published by Regal Books, a division of Gospel Light, Ventura, CA.

Transcribed tapes of Beth Alves:

The Cost of Discipling
Mentoring Children In Prayer

Websites:

http://www.intercessorsinternational.org/nav.htm
http://www.intercessorsinternational.org/beth.htm

Chapter 10

Shelter of the Swallow

Of all the men and women in the Bible who came to know God intimately, David was certainly one who understood what it meant to enter the secret place of the Holy Spirit. In Psalm 84, David paints a sensitive and inviting word picture for us.

> How lovely are your tabernacles, O Lord of hosts! My soul yearns, yes, even pines and is homesick for the courts of the Lord; my heart and my flesh cry out and sing for joy to the living God. Yes, the sparrow has found a house, and the swallow a nest for herself, where she may lay her young—even Your altars, O Lord of hosts, my King and my God.

> Blessed (happy, fortunate, to be envied) are those who dwell in Your house and Your presence; they will be singing Your praises all the day long. Selah [pause, and calmly think of that]! Passing through the Valley of Weeping (Baca), they make a place of springs; the early rain also fills [the pools] with blessings. They go from strength to strength [increasing in victorious power]; each of them appears before God in Zion.

*For a day in Your courts is better than a thousand [any-
where else]; I would rather be a doorkeeper and stand at
the threshold in the house of my God than to dwell [at
ease] in the tents of wickedness* (AMP).

Recently, when I read this wonderful psalm I was in a
quiet and reflective mood with the Lord. I felt Him drawing my
attention to verse 3: "Yes, the sparrow has found a house, and
the swallow a nest for herself, where she may lay her young—
even Your altars, O Lord of hosts, my King and my God."

This Scripture is one of my most treasured possessions!
It was treasured by my grandmother and then by my mother.
It has become part of my family heritage. The more Scripture
we have hidden away in our hearts the greater the opportunity we give to God to speak into our beings. I have one such
experience I'd like to share with you.

My girls and I were over at our neighbor's place where
they were taking riding lessons. As the horses were being
brought in, groomed, and saddled up, I was enjoying myself
by watching everyone and all the animals. I happened to look
up and see a barn swallow's nest built against the rafters of
the barn. *What a delightful find!* I thought to myself.

My excitement was genuine for my mother had been
quite a bird watcher and had taught me to highly value these
beautiful creatures for their unique qualities.

Personally, I think that barn swallows are some of the
most beautiful birds in God's creation. They have such an iri-
descent bluish, black coloring on their backs, and their faces,
throats, and breasts are rich shades of deep orange. These precious little creatures perform like flying acrobats as they
swoop and dive after insects in the early evening light.

As I stood there admiring these fascinating little birds, the Lord began to weave together for me an understanding of Psalm 84 using these beautiful swallows. I found myself thinking what an accurate picture David had painted concerning their nature, especially when building their nests.

A swallow will first find a structure where there is a supply of mud close by. It will carry mud and twigs in its little beak, making trip after trip. Then it carefully constructs its nest, placing the mud on a board up close to the ceiling of the barn, creating a mud-dauber type of structure. The outside of the nest is very solid and very secure. Yet, the inside of the nest is lined with down feathers and is soft, warm, and inviting!

There is an understanding of the way of wisdom that God has deposited within His creation. In animals we call it "instinct." How do the birds know to fly south for the winter? Where do they get their sense of when it is time to start their migration? How do they know which way to go, covering hundreds of miles every year? They don't deal with "fears," or "the flesh." They were created with the "knowing" that these things are the right and safe things to do.

The thought struck me: *Swallows build their nests the way they do because, instinctively, they know that the safest place to build is up against the wall*. On the other hand, we use the expression "up against the wall" to describe a place of inner struggle where we may feel trapped or feel that we've run out of options, and we have no place to run and no way out.

We as human beings don't have instinct deposited within us, apart from the Holy Spirit. Instead, God leaves us to make our choices, having shown us in His Word the narrow road to follow. Our mistakes and failures have left scars of fear and anxiety, which cause us to think running away will keep us safe. Oh, that we would learn from the swallow the wisdom of God, that we would let our Divine Shepherd's leading and guiding become so deep in us so as to mirror the powerful instincts built within His creation. May He build within the fabric of our lives the truth that the place of abiding is found where difficulty crosses our will and our fear. That is actually the safest place.

To quote an old and wise saying: "Going to the cross is going to the point where my will crosses God's will." How desperately we need to abide in God by staying close to the cross!

When We Are Weak...

Throughout this book, we've been looking at the lessons we can learn from some of history's great Christian women, women who knew how to enter the secret place of the Most High. Certainly, their lives were not easy. These women were not even "natural born saints." They went through trials, persecutions, and testings, just as we do. We all have a tendency to look back on the life of someone who passed the test, who walked mightily with God, and think, *There must have been something different about her. Somehow it was easier for that individual to choose God than it is for me.*

I don't believe that for one minute!

Each one of us must go to the cross. There are no exceptions. The cross is the place where our will and God's will cross each other. The cross is always the place where God's will stands before me, the place I want to run from as fast and far as I can.

But you see, that's the point where God will meet us—where we are spiritually weakest. It's also the point at which He will give us His grace and strength in place of our weakness.

The truth is, God has a cross that is designed perfectly for each one of us. He knows the details of our lives, and He knows exactly how to direct us into situations where our natural strength is tested. He knows how to apply pressure so that every natural desire—that force in us that wants to cling to everything that is not Him—can be exposed for the idolatry it is.

Spiritual storms, winds, and billows will blow into our lives, pulling us this way and that. We become like swallows tossed around on gale winds and feel torn about which way we want to go. We plead with Him—or rail at Him—to make the storm winds stop. Nevertheless, we find the testing gets tougher.

Sometimes, while in the face of winds and danger, we know there is a place of safety in God, but still we don't fly to that safe place in Him. Instead, we fly away, resisting the wisdom that tells us to fly to Him. We know in our spirits what flying towards Him will mean. We know it will require first going to the cross.

Yes, in God are found peace, safety, comfort, rest; but testing and discomfort are also woven into His design. And running towards what is uncomfortable is exactly where we are going to find Him. Only after that will we find our rest. This is why David tells us in Psalm 84 to fly to that place in God—the secret place of our greatest testing, known to God and us alone. Contrary to every natural feeling, contrary to what the world tells us about seeking comfort and ease, we are to make our nest there. As we abide in this place, we build history with God. Every trial and difficulty and fearful thing He brings us through becomes a part of the nest He has prepared for us. Day by day, He lines our nest with His faithfulness, His goodness, His mercy. We rest secure in this strong tower, so soft and warm.

I believe that if we will not run from that place, but fly to the cross God has prepared for us, then we will find all the provision and safety for which we long. Where we are weakest He will be strong.

Where She May Lay Her Young

David said, "Yes, the sparrow has found a house, and the swallow a nest for herself, where she may lay her young—even Your altars, O Lord of hosts, my King and my God." We can rest our young in the shelter of that holy, wonderful presence, also. It doesn't matter if our young happens to be our children, our dreams, our goals, our ministries, our gifts.

This shelter, this nest is not for us alone. It's also a place for those concerns in our lives that matter most to us. There our fragile, tender, developing "young" can be nurtured and protected under the loving wings of God.

Where Is Your Nest?

A few days after rediscovering this psalm, I was still thinking about this whole business of swallows, the psalms, and the cross. I was outside our office, trimming branches from one of our trees. As I brought my blade up underneath some branches, I found another bird's nest.

This nest was nothing like the sturdy swallows' nest in the barn. It was lying sort of haphazardly on a couple of dead, weak branches. The nest itself was really, really small, and very flimsy. It was made of some dried grasses and not much else.

Immediately, I thought: *This is the way most of us build nests. We pick the weakest sight—trusting in fickle people who change, or in possessions that break, or in jobs and positions that can be taken from us. We look for our greatest security where there really is no security.*

Not only that, but we build out of the flimsiest materials. We base our sense of well-being on how we feel, on current opinions, and on what this or that trendy expert on a daytime talk show advises—fluff that the world has to offer.

On our own, apart from the Lord, we don't know how to build a nest that's secure. We don't know where our hiding place is a lot of times. Too often we wait until difficulty comes, and we frantically try to throw together a nest—a piece of homespun philosophy here, what Oprah said there—anything to grasp at security. It's like the flimsy little nest I discovered on two dead branches outside our office. Some of us even convince ourselves that we're doing okay all on our own. What we've latched onto seems good; but there is a big problem: The nests of security we build out of what the world has to offer are not anchored. They offer no real security, only the illusion of it. When the wind comes that flimsy little nest will fall. Security of our own making grants us no real abiding place.

I am not pointing any fingers here, because we're all guilty. We all start out wanting to find our security in things, people, and positions of power or honor. As Christians we look for security in our church, our Christian friends, or in our identity as a Bible study leader. Many of us women find our security in our identity as a wife or mother.

What we need is a place for our spirit that is solid and secure. God's Word is filled with assurances that He wants to be a shelter for us in times of trouble. He wants to be our rock (see Ps. 92), our fortress (see Ps. 18), and our strong tower (see Prov. 18). These are all good images of places to where we can flee when danger has come upon us and we need a temporary hiding place. Yet, these are not intended as places to live for a long time.

What's so wonderful about David's imagery in Psalm 84 is that a *nest* is more than an emergency shelter. A nest is where you can live always. Here you can abide in peace when everything around us is being shaken or everything around you is still.

Where is your nest? What do you trust in for your security, peace, and strength? If you know the Lord as your God and Savior—has He become for you a nest where your spirit can flee to find the shelter it needs?

Softly and Tenderly

As children in Sunday school, we sang, "Softly and Tenderly Jesus is Calling." He called the apostle John in the Book of the Revelation to "come up here." From the deep He called deeply and drew David's panting, longing heart to His presence. Throughout the ages and centuries He called, and one by one they came—Madam Guyon, Teresa of Avila, Fanny Crosby, Susanna Wesley, Gwen Shaw, Beth Alves. With longing hearts and passionate desire, they were drawn to His secret place.

If you get quiet enough and listen, you'll hear Him calling you, too. Yes, the sparrow has found a house, and the swallow a nest for herself. David and so many others found their rest at the altars of the Lord. And now it's your turn. Softly, tenderly, quietly He's calling you from the depths of His wonderful presence. How will you respond? Will you join Him in the secret place?

> *Dear Heavenly Father, I come to You in the name of Jesus, Your Son. I am longing to enter a deeper place of fellowship with You, but I'm not quite sure I know how to get there. Help me find my secret place to meet with You. Help me open up the room in my heart that is meant for only You and me together, forever! Let me hear the song You are singing over the mountains, trying to reach my heart. Give me the song to sing that will so bless Your heart, and bring You great joy. Lord, come, and take all the bits and pieces of my life and my heart, and make it into a beautiful symphony of love of devotion to You! I love You! In Jesus Name,* Amen.

Coming soon from
Jim W. Goll

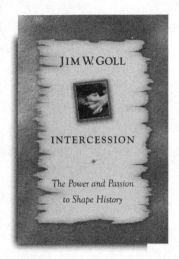

INTERCESSION

The Power and Passion to Shape History

The words of an intercessor are a powerful force for healing the wounds of the past and shaping the course of history. This book helps the intercessor release those words into the heavens and bring down God's healing results on earth. Goll shifts the focus of intercession away from the typical "shotgun" approach of praying for the whole world in a single prayer while portraying how you can focus your prayer on what God desires.

ISBN 0-7684-2184-5

Also by
Jim W. and Michal Ann Goll

THE LOST ART OF INTERCESSION
by Jim W. Goll.
Finally there is something that really explains what is happening to so many folk in the Body of Christ. What does it mean to carry the burden of the Lord? Where is it in Scripture and in history? Why do I feel as though God is groaning within me? No, you are not crazy; God is restoring genuine intercessory prayer in the hearts of those who are open to respond to His burden and His passion.
ISBN 1-56043-697-2

ENCOUNTERS WITH A SUPERNATURAL GOD
by Jim W. and Michal Ann Goll.
The Golls know that angels are real. They have firsthand experience with supernatural angelic encounters. In this book you'll read and learn about angels and supernatural manifestations of God's Presence—and the real encounters that both Jim and Michal Ann have had! As the founders of Ministry to the Nations and speakers and teachers, they share that God wants to be intimate friends with His people. Go on an adventure with the Golls and find out if God has a supernatural encounter for you!
ISBN 1-56043-199-7

WOMEN ON THE FRONT LINES
by Michal Ann Goll.
History is filled with ordinary women who have changed the course of their generation. Here Michal Ann Goll, co-founder of Ministry to the Nations with her husband, Jim, shares how her own life was transformed and highlights nine women whose lives will impact yours! Every generation faces the same choices and issues; learn how you, too, can heed the call to courage and impact a generation.
ISBN 0-7684-2020-2

Available at your local Christian bookstore.

For more information and sample chapters, visit www.destinyimage.com

Additional copies of this book and other
book titles from DESTINY IMAGE are
available at your local bookstore.

For a complete list of our titles,
visit us at www.destinyimage.com
Send a request for a catalog to:

Destiny Image® Publishers, Inc.

P.O. Box 310
Shippensburg, PA 17257-0310

*"Speaking to the Purposes of God for This
Generation and for the Generations to Come"*